RED FLAGS

in

KEY WEST

A true story about love and lies

Red Flags in Key West
Copyright © 2023
by Kimberly Rae Owens

Disclaimer

This is a memoir based on actual events. Some
names, locations, and dates may have been changed
to protect the privacy of individuals.

ISBN: 979-8-218-30149-1
Printed in the United States of America

Cover design by Kimberly Rae Owens
Portrait by Diana Johnson Photography
Edited by Kristen Rae Ponder

Amazon Kindle Direct Publishing
https://kdp.amazon.com

Dedications

I'd like to dedicate this book to all the single ladies out there looking for love. Do not ignore your gut feelings and take notice of the RED FLAGS. Listen to your family and friends because they are usually right. People on the outside of the situation can see what we don't want to see. We tend to wear our 'love' blinders that fog up and obscure the truth. We need to learn to love ourselves first before diving in too deep.

Acknowledgements

First, I want to thank God for always being there and watching over me every step of the way, and for giving me the sign that I needed when I needed it. And for leading me to write this book to tell my story.

I want to thank my three daughters, Tara, Kristen, and Megan for supporting me and helping me with some of my editing. A special thanks to Kristen who has helped me the most, even while she was going through her own issues. I appreciate all your help and patience with me. I also know it wasn't easy for you girls to read what your mom went through. I thank each of you for the understanding and for the support I needed. I have the best daughters ever! I love you!

A special thanks to my parents for always being there and supporting me. I know you worry about me in all my adventures, but you are always by my side no matter what. That means the world to me, and I love you for that. And I made sure you got your Key Lime pie!

All my friends who were there for me throughout this whole experience deserve a huge thank you, especially Kim (Julia), who was there first-hand since we were roommates. Some of you were skeptical from the get-go and kept telling me he wasn't for real. The more I heard those words, the more I dove in and wanted to prove to you otherwise. It's hard to admit when you are wrong and to accept

failure, and then face everyone afterwards. But you were there for me no matter what and I love you all for that. I will try my best to listen to you next time.

I want to thank all the locals in Key West that I came in contact with and that I am now friends with. Without your help I would have so many more unanswered questions. You helped me to realize that I wasn't so crazy after all. I enjoyed meeting all of you and I hope our paths will cross again next time I'm in Key West.

While working night shift, God put me in the path of Lance Brazelton. Lance has published two books and is currently working on another children's book series. Lance has walked me through some of the steps on how to self-publish a book. I want to thank Lance for steering me in the right direction, because I was totally clueless before.

I'd like to thank my work family at Madison Hospital. You all have been my encouraging, supportive cheerleaders while I've been writing this book this past year. You have no idea how much you all mean to me. I love each and every one of you!

I have made some lifelong friends throughout this journey and would like to thank them for helping me fill in some of the missing pieces. Without your insight, I may not have discovered the truth.

Lastly, I want to thank all the writers out there. I had no idea how hard it was to write a book! Without the help from the internet, I'm not sure I'd even have a

book. I learned a lot and I am thankful for all you talented writers to keep our minds entertained and learning from your words. Even though this book isn't even close to a novel, it is my experience and my words and I'm hoping anyone who reads it will at least slightly understand what I went through. If it helps one person in any way, then all the hard work and time was worth every second.

Contents

Dedications..iii

Acknowledgements.......................................v

01. Solo Trip...1

02. Key Lime Pie....................................17

03. Fantasy Fest.....................................31

04. Downsizing......................................53

05. Florida...63

06. Key West...77

07. Marinas...85

08. Maggots...105

09. I Love You.......................................115

10. Sailing...127

11. Marathon...143

12. Alabama..153

13. Tickets..159

14. Mother's Day....................................165

15. Apartment Building 171

16. Panic Attack.....................................185

17. Lies..199

18. One Way Ticket.................................211

19. Not Over..231

20. Confrontation....................................247

21. Epilogue..265

22. About the Author...............................275

Chapter 1

(Solo Trip)

It was the seventh summer after my divorce of a twenty-six-year marriage, and one year after a break-up of two and a half years, that I truly found myself.

That spring was also an ending of a long-time friendship that was upsetting. After that, I knew it was time for me to move forward. So, from that day on, I let go of all the negative things in my life and decided to live life to the fullest and to challenge myself to new adventures.

Earlier in the year I had already accomplished many little feats, so my new plan was to go on my first solo trip to Key West, Florida and stay on a sailboat at Stock Island through Airbnb. I decided that I was not waiting anymore for that right person to go with me, I was proceeding to go on my own. It was time for some self-reflecting. It had been years since I'd been to Key West, and I was looking forward to being back at the Southernmost point of the U.S. Key West is a two-mile by four-mile tropical island. Florida was my home for sixteen years at one time and all three of my girls were born and raised there, so it has a special place in my heart. It's like home to me, even though I was born and raised in Oregon. I've had some struggles over the years with all my family on the West Coast besides my three daughters, but I wouldn't trade them for anything. That's what happens when you leave home at twenty to join the army.

I called my friend Cookie to tell her of my plans for my solo trip and I added that I was planning on sky diving while in the Keys. My plane was already booked, so it was undoubtedly going to happen!

"You know I'm only four hours away from Key West!" she replied.

I said, "Come on then, but let me have the first two days to myself, I need to know what it's like to be a tourist on my own." And it was true. Of all the trips I'd ever taken, all of them I was with someone, whether it was with my family or friends. This new chapter in my life was all about me and figuring out who I was. I couldn't do that if I went on a trip and went along with what someone else wanted to do the entire time.

I also contacted another friend named Casey from the town I lived at in Alabama, who was at that time living down in Sugarloaf Key. I informed Casey of my plans and she said she'd stop by the Marina that I was going to be staying at for a visit. All the planning was working out perfectly, and I couldn't wait! As soon as I could, I started packing and planning my whole trip of what I wanted to do. I got really excited finding different events and things to do during the time I was going to be down there.

After landing in Key West on June 30th, 2021, I acquired an Uber and couldn't wait to see what the sailboat was going to look like as my sleeping quarters. After being dropped off at the marina, I followed the directions the owner gave me and walked past all these amazing yachts and sailboats. I had only ever been on a sailboat a couple times in my life, and they were nothing compared to these boats. I thought I hit the jackpot and would be living like a Queen for a few nights and became more and more excited. After walking past all these great-looking vessels, I was a little disappointed when I found my boat, "Connecting the Dots." It was one of the smaller ones that looked a little rough on the edges. All the positive reviews said how they loved it and how clean it was, so I shrugged my shoulders and thought if the reviews and pictures were nice, it didn't have to be as big as the other boats I saw. I had high hopes it would still be fun.

After meeting the owner and him showing me my side of the boat, it wasn't so bad after all. A huge bed, a tiny bathroom, and some shelves on both sides. It was air-conditioned and clean like the reviews said, which was good enough for me. If I could have only figured out how to use the toilet. I wasn't used to a toilet having directions. Living on a boat was a whole different lifestyle. My room was 102, and the owner lived in 101. There was a wall in-between us, made just for Airbnb guests. I later found out the owner had bought the boat off Craig's List just to rent it. He had never even sailed on it.

After getting my stuff aboard the boat and all settled in, I decided to check out my surroundings. It was an amazing first day already and I was feeling fantastic. I explored the marina I was staying at, noticing tourists and locals using their bicycles as a means of transportation. Everyone was friendly and welcomed me as I passed them by.

Casey, her husband, their son, and Casey's son's girlfriend stopped by to have a drink with me at the restaurant that was in the marina. We had some great conversations and they invited me and Cookie to go out on their pontoon boat before our skydiving adventure. All of that sounded like a perfect day ahead of us.

I was tired from all the excitement and decided to call it a night after they left. I had my first night of sleeping on a sailboat, and all by myself! That new chapter in my life was starting off great and I was exhilarated. I was entering new territory of doing things by myself and for myself, and I loved it. That night had a feeling of satisfaction about it as I laid my head down to sleep.

The next morning, I mapped out a four-mile run into Key West to finish at the Southernmost Point. I was training for a trail run back in Alabama, so a four-mile run would be perfect. Double-checking the map, I grabbed a few dollars and my phone and went off into Key West. With it being July, the weather was very hot and humid, but I didn't mind since I enjoyed the heat. It did make me sweat, though, making the run a very satisfying workout that kicked in even more happy hormones. I was on cloud nine thinking about where I was in my life: I was doing whatever I wanted, when I wanted, in a city I've never been to alone before, confident, and with no kids or partner to say otherwise. I felt great! Before I knew it, I was at the

Southernmost point, enjoying the views, drenched in sweat, and catching my breath.

After I took a few pictures at the Southernmost point icon, it was time for a snack and to figure out how I was going to get back to the boat. I needed to shower and change clothes for the rest of the day. Grabbing some fruit and lots of water, I sat down and thought about my options and settled on renting a bicycle for a few hours. What better way to explore the city on my way back to the boat than to live like a local. Plus, Cookie was coming into town that night and we could use her car, so I didn't need something for very long. When I was done with my little break and feeding the chickens that were roaming, I headed to my bike.

I hopped on the bicycle and realized how tired my legs were. I started thinking to myself, why didn't I rent a scooter instead? What was I thinking? My confidence started to lower slightly. Once I started pedaling it wasn't so bad, and I was able to see the sea life while riding next to the ocean. While going over the bridge into Stock Island, I received a sweet surprise: a group of Sand sharks feeding off fish. That definitely solidified that I was not in Alabama anymore! In fact, I felt like I was at an aquarium. I had to call my mom and dad at that moment to share in the excitement.

When I started heading back again, I almost ran over multiple small lizards and saw some sizeable iguanas skirt away. I knew I would never have seen any of that if I rented a scooter, so I felt better about my decision. I felt invigorated and like I was a local riding my bike with a basket on the front, and I probably looked like one if only it didn't say RENT ME in huge bold letters on the front! Either way, I was in heaven.

I finally made it back to the boat and grabbed my personal items to take a shower across the sidewalk at the community bathroom. The bathroom on the boat was very tiny and since I wasn't quite sure how to pump the toilet correctly, I didn't want to risk messing up the shower. Going to a bathroom I knew how to use was the best option. It had a tiled shower, and the door was open at the top so you could experience the beautiful outdoors while cleaning up.

After my shower I put on my sundress and hat and hopped back on the bike to head back into Key West, this time choosing the other side of the island. A little different scenery but just as beautiful. It was then time for lunch, and I asked a local where the best place to eat a fish sandwich would be. When I found it, I parked my bike and was excited to have my first shrimp roll at D.J.'s Clam Shack. The local told me it had been featured on the show *Diners, Drive-Ins, & Dives*, so it had to be good. I was very pleased once again with my decision; it was delicious, and the environment was fun.

Sooner than I would have liked, it was time to turn in my bike. My next stop was the famous Duval Street, and it was without a doubt time for a beer at Sloppy Joe's. While enjoying my drink, I ended up chatting with a group of men that were on a weekend trip. Everyone was so friendly and happy, and they all seemed to be on vacation. After my beer I wandered over to Hog's Breath Saloon, then some tourist shops while making my way to Mallory Square where everyone watches the sunset. I wanted a good spot to watch the sun go down over the ocean, so I kept on walking and made it to a tiny beach and small pier. It was the perfect location, and I even helped a guy hold one of his fishing poles while he pulled in a fish with his other one.

The sunsets in Key West were breathtaking and I was enjoying every second of that particular one's descent. The colors became even more vivid after the sun disappeared over the horizon. All the pictures I took didn't seem to do it justice. The beauty of the clear sky, bright colors, and ocean smell made it where I didn't want to leave. If only time could slow down to make it last a little longer. I was mesmerized and felt at peace with where I was at in life.

After the sun was completely down and I started heading back, I realized that just around the corner was Kermit's Key Lime Pie shop. That was a sign! I had to get a piece of pie while waiting for Cookie to pick me up and take me back to the boat. I told her I'd be the girl sitting on the curb eating a piece of Key Lime Pie.

While I was waiting and eating my pie, I was reflecting on the most amazing day I have had in such a long time. I was truly at peace with myself and who I've become. It's been a journey finding myself after being lost in a long marriage, and that journey was still going. In that twenty-six year marriage, I basically forgot who I was. Being a wife and a mom were great and I loved those roles, but those roles consumed me, and I lost who I was in those years. Being by myself that day, I was able to be who I wanted to be, and I wanted to be free and fun and alive! Niki Rae was finally showing up for herself and it felt great. Being in Key West all by myself was so refreshing and I was enjoying every moment. It was July 1st, the day I showed up for myself and I was proud. The sun had set, my stomach was full, I met some incredible people, my legs were tired, and there was my ride.

Cookie drove four and half hours to see me and I had a packed day with lots of exercise, so we both decided to just have a drink at the boat that night. The next day we had a full schedule and wanted to be rested and ready to start the day off right.

Cookie has been like a sister to me ever since her and her family moved in across the street from us in Vero Beach, Florida, when my twins were born twenty-seven years ago. We both have been through a lot and seem to have the same spirit. We were more like Soul Sisters.

Our principles are the same: to play hard and love even harder. Neither one of us ever seemed to get it right though, yet even with all the heartbreaks we've experienced, we never stop trying. We encourage each other in just about every aspect of our lives and both of us know we can turn to the other in hard times. That's why it was so great that we have each other. We laugh, we cry, we get drunk. I really don't know what I'd do without her.

After some catching up and a good night's sleep, the next morning we drove to Sugarloaf Key to go on the pontoon boat ride with Casey and her family. We ended up snorkeling with stingrays, fish, and man of wars. The water was incredible with so many shades of blue. They took us out to an island, snorkeled some more, then headed back while watching a funnel cloud in the distance. We had the most wonderful time, but it was then time to get ready for our skydiving adventure. We said our goodbyes and thanked Casey and her family for inviting us.

Cookie and I changed in the car, drove about a half mile down the road, crossed the street, and within minutes we were in a small airplane gaining altitude before skydiving out! We were literally just in the water below us snorkeling and riding in a pontoon boat. We went from land to water to air. "Who does that?" we asked ourselves. We burst out laughing, then answered, "We do!" Seeing the keys from a bird's eye view at 10,000 feet was spectacular! It was the best day ever! Our adrenaline was pumping, and we were on top of the world!

After landing and watching the videos and laughing our asses off, we headed back to Stock Island to find someplace to eat. We said that next time we were going to jump with a full bodysuit so the videos will not capture all our skin flapping around. Neither one of us purchased those videos because of that. We laughed so hard we had tears coming down.

When we were done eating, laughing, and sharing our experiences and getting the knots out of our hair, we got ready to make an evening of Key West. We were ready to make that town our own and nobody could stop the natural high we were on.

We rushed into town, and we were more than ready to continue celebrating this most amazing day that we were already having. After much giggling and a couple drinks in, we decided to walk on the boardwalk next to the pier. It was a lively evening with all the tourists and locals bustling by. It was easy to fall into the rhythm of the crowd. We rounded the corner and in front of us was a fancy Resort that blocked our way from walking by the water unless you were staying there. Cookie decided to start a conversation with the security guy in the booth. He was very funny and the people staying at the resort walking by appreciated his humor. I asked him if he ever left the security box, and he came back with some witty answer that made me laugh. We chatted with him for a bit, and I noticed how our personalities meshed. We had fun joking and talking to all the tourists coming and going from the resort. His personality was very attractive to me, plus he was charming.

An Uber pulled up dropping some people off and we noticed it had a disco ball hanging from the ceiling in it. The whole car was lit up on the inside with 70's music playing.

Cookie says, "I want to ride in an Uber like that!" I agreed; it looked like a traveling party!

The security guy heard her and told us to wait a minute, so he ran over to the car and retrieved their number for us.

He handed me the piece of paper and said, "Here's their number, and here's my number!" His name was Chad.

The night was young, and we needed to move on to Duval Street where the town was bustling with tourists and partygoers. When we said bye to Chad, he invited us to come back at midnight when he was off his shift, and he'd let us in the pool at the resort. We told him thank you, but we were on the fence about what we were going to do; the evening was ours and it was time to press forward to do our own thing.

Walking around town, we stopped for a drink and somehow got picked up by a couple and a single guy who was sweet on Cookie. He was tall and cute, and they looked good together. He took her hand and made us follow him to find the smallest bar in Key West. Here we go on another adventure!

After what seemed like an eternity, we finally found the smallest bar in Key West. We may have even passed it a few times since it was so small. A little while after some conversation, our new friend went up to the bar to get us a drink and a group of young fellows told Cookie that her husband was hilarious.

We both laughed and she said, "I don't even know what his name is!" Everyone roared with laughter.

Our little group soon grew into a much bigger group with the new guys, and off we went to find a place to do some dancing. They knew exactly where to take us, and we had so much fun. All the guys were very entertaining and respected us to where we didn't have to worry. We stayed in that group until they all disappeared one by one. By that time, we met some Irish men who had scooters that let us ride them in the street. Cookie and I were zipping up and down Duval Street like we owned it. It seemed like nobody was on the road but us, and it made for some great pictures since there was no one around.

Not long after that, the tiredness hit us, and it was time to call an Uber to take us back to Stock Island. We needed to get a few hours of sleep before making our journeys back home. Unfortunately, the Uber ride did not have a disco ball hanging from the ceiling like we wanted, but it did have a clock on the dashboard that read 4:50a.m.! Holy Moly! We really DID own Duval Street! No wonder it seemed like we were the only ones on the street. It's because we really were. What an adrenaline rush.

Making it back to the boat, we barely made it onto the bed before passing out. A few hours later, Cookie was getting a phone call to have breakfast with one of the guys she met. Since she was going to do her thing for breakfast, I rummaged through my stuff to find the piece of paper with Chad's number on it and decided to give him a call.

When he answered, I said, "Good morning, this is Niki Rae. I was wondering if you'd like to come hang out at the pool with me before I head back to Alabama today."

He said, "I was hoping that you would call. I waited till 1:00am for you to show back up at the hotel. I could have gotten a room for you and your girlfriend. But I'm glad you called, I will hop on my bike and be there soon."

When Chad arrived, he was cuter and taller than I remembered. I was a little nervous all of a sudden, but in a good way. The beach look suited him, with his tan skin, khaki shorts, a Patagonia t-shirt, Costa sunglasses and reef flip flops; I liked it. As he was walking toward me, he saw I was getting my luggage out of the sailboat, and he jumped to help.

Before Cookie left for her date, she was at her car cleaning it out, and she came up to me to hand me my bathing suit and cover up saying I might need them. Chad looked at me with a confused expression, and I knew exactly what he was thinking. Sure enough, he asked me if I stayed with someone. Of course, I did not, and I told him that those were left in her car from snorkeling the day before. Why would I have called him if I was with someone else? Also, why was I defending myself to a guy I just met? (This could have been my first Red Flag). He left it alone and we made our way to the pool to chill out while Cookie took off to go on her breakfast date.

The pool was packed with tourists, and we joined right in. We found a corner in the pool that was unoccupied. It was a perfect place to talk and get to know each other. He said if I came back, he would take me to a private island for dinner, then we could scuba dive, go snorkeling or do whatever I wanted. I kept a grin on my face because it all seemed too good. Chad seemed to be just as into me as I was into him. His eyes were intense and the reflection off the pool water seemed to turn his hazel eyes blue. I felt like I could drown in his eyes. I also loved listening to him talk with his New Jersey accent. I was so engulfed in his eyes and voice while we were in the pool that I barely heard what he had to say. He was so hypnotizing that I was having a hard time focusing. Luckily, I didn't have to say too much since he did most of the talking.

He told me his mom was German but passed away too young, and he was adopted by an Italian family. When he was old enough, he left to join the military and ended up a Ranger and retiring after twenty years. After that he lived in the Adirondacks and built a cabin while living in a trailer. He lived there with his dog before moving down to Key West. It was information overload, (and probably my second Red Flag). I couldn't keep it all straight, plus I was feeling a little lightheaded from only a few hours of sleep. It was a lot to take in, but I was enjoying it, nonetheless. He was all smiles, very charming and only forty-four years old and liking me at fifty-five years old. So why wouldn't I like this guy? I told him a little about myself; having three beautiful daughters, working in a hospital as a Respiratory Therapist and I liked doing wood working. He was super impressed with everything and kept telling me to come back and see him.

We got out of the pool to take a walk on the beach, and he tried to hold my hand, but it felt a little awkward, so I pulled away. I wasn't used to anyone being so forward, although I was enjoying every second; I also liked how he would talk and be polite to everyone around us. He had the kind of personality I loved in a man.

Just around the corner there was a little boy and girl gazing at a dead crab. Chad walked up to them, and, with a soft voice, he explained to them that a female crab would lay its eggs and then crawl up on a rock, look up at the moon and then die. He picked up the dead crab, turned it over, and showed them how he knew it was a female. His knowledge and kindness fascinated me. We walked further along the water, and he would point out the different sea life and tell me their names and history. Working in an aquarium helped with his expertise about sea life.

Chad made me feel at ease with his easygoing conversations and positive outlook on life. I was enjoying the little time we had together.

By the time we got back to the pool, Cookie was already there waiting on us. It was time for her to take me to the airport. I went into the bathroom, changed into a sundress, combed out my saltwater hair and put my wet clothes in a bag. Cookie and Chad were making small talk when I walked out. Cookie was nice enough to leave Chad and I alone for a few minutes so we could say our goodbyes. We decided to stay in touch and exchanged numbers. Just before I turned to leave, he gave me a kiss I wouldn't forget, with a tight, long hug to follow. My face was blushed, and I couldn't stop smiling. He watched us leave and waved goodbye. I asked Cookie how her breakfast date went, and she replied that he was just another player, and she was hoping he would have been more like Chad.

Cookie dropped me off and I found my way to my boarding area. Chad started texting me while I was waiting for the plane to take off. He was saying that he would be waving as I flew past his place and would be waiting for my return. Cookie texted me saying she couldn't stop smiling, that it was the best weekend ever. I totally agreed. It had been a long time since I've felt that free, relaxed, and happy. We were going back into our busy lives with full hearts.

It was July 6th, and I was back to work, but this time I was refreshed and was even told that I was glowing. Key West was definitely good for me, and I definitely wanted to go back.

Chapter 2

(Key Lime Pie)

Chad and I were texting back and forth quite often after I made it back home. He even said that he knew I'd be someone that he could fall in love with. It was all so fresh that I was a little skeptical at that point, but I enjoyed hearing it from him, especially when I felt the same way. It felt good to have someone saying so many kind words to me. We seemed to be texting each other on a regular basis. I told him that I was wanting to retire to the beach one day and buy a duplex so I could live on one side and do Airbnb on the other side. He was intrigued and added how we could do it together. I never had a partner go along with my dreams as a team to accomplish them together. It was a new feeling, like a breath of fresh air. Then shortly after, conversations seemed to center around him (RED FLAG).

One afternoon I heard from Chad, and he was all excited to tell me that while he was working at the hotel, everyone started yelling because a child was drowning in the ocean, so he ran, dove in, and saved the child. He said that as he was walking back to the hotel everyone was cheering from their balconies for him. I wasn't sure to believe it or not. He heard the doubt in my voice and reassured me that he was in Key West and that things like that happened there. Who was I to not believe? (RED FLAG)

We moved on to talking about everyday life. He explained to me how he saved fish and donated them to the local pet stores, and that he had multiple fish tanks at his condo. He told me how he would go out to the islands with his buddies and do some spear fishing for fresh fish and lobster for dinner. I quickly learned that he loved to cook and wanted me to join him on his fishing trips just so he could make me one of his best meals, after scuba diving, of course. Then he said we could possibly camp on the island and fall asleep while watching the stars. It all sounded so exciting and wonderful. How could I not want to see him again?

Chad also said that I wouldn't have liked him two years ago; he was about one hundred pounds heavier. After drinking all the time and gaining weight, he decided to stop drinking and exercise more. Since then, he would ride his bike thirty miles a day and only worked for fun, because he was also bored; hence the weight gain. He never touched his pension from the military because he had money coming in from rental property up North, so after retiring from the military he never really had to work.

I said, "So you have Tricare then?" (The military insurance).

He said, "Yes, I have three insurances."

I was confused and said, "Why would you have three insurances?"

"You can never be too cautious," He replied.

I was thinking, well okay then, that's odd, but to each his own, and I never thought about it after that (RED FLAG).

There was a YouTube video Chad uploaded about how he cooked for all the locals in Key West during hurricane Irma that he wanted me to see. I watched it and I saw how he was heavier back then just like he said, but he was still a good-looking guy. His video talked about all the meat he was cooking that was donated from Harpoon Harry's since the power went out. It showed him in a backyard of a house. I scrolled through other videos he uploaded, and one was about his dog he had mentioned before, and a couple of them in a garage with a BMW and a boat motor he was trying to sell. I tried looking him up on social media but was unable to find anything on him. He had already told me he didn't do social media, I had to look anyways. He told me that the house in the video was his, and later he decided to rent it out to some of his buddies who needed a place to stay. That's why he was living in a condo.

Chad always had some stories to tell that would lead to helping the homeless or donating his fish or his time to Key West (Red Flag). It seemed to me that he was bragging at times, but I didn't think too much of it. I had a hard time keeping up with his childhood the most since there were so many stories he would tell and so many places he named. I would mention my family and upbringing, but soon the conversations would shift back to him. It didn't bother me as much at first because I enjoyed hearing all these stories and life experiences. Hearing about

19

other people's lives really interests me, and I was more than intrigued.

I had a quick trip planned to see my parents for a long weekend in Seattle starting July 14th. When I arrived, I couldn't stop telling my mom all about Chad. We even looked up the video he had posted on YouTube about hurricane Irma. She said he seemed like a good guy. I told Chad I was in Seattle visiting my parents and he said he wanted to overnight them a key lime pie from Kermit's there in Key West. I thought that was the sweetest thing and was on board. I gave him their address and he said it would be delivered soon. I was thrilled that this guy was spending the time and money to impress me and my parents, and what an awesome thing to get so close to my dad's birthday.

The next day came and went with no pie. I asked Chad if he gave the correct address. He said he would go to Kermit's and double check it. He let me know everything was good and that it should be arriving since he paid over $100.00 for that pie. I finally told my parents about the pie and so they started checking their mail and the front porch regularly. They said that occasionally their mail goes to another address that is very similar to theirs, so we were thinking that someone else was enjoying their pie. Every time I mentioned it to Chad, he would say he would go talk to Kermit and find out what happened. I never did get a real answer from Chad, and mom and dad never received any key lime pie (RED FLAG).

20

It was July 19th, and I was back in Alabama planning a road trip to see Cookie over Labor Day weekend. Chad and I were trying to figure out how I could take a couple days to drive on down to Key West from her house to spend some time together since I'd be so close. He would take me to all the places he had been talking about. That was something to look forward to.

A few days went by without hearing from Chad, and I was getting a little worried. He finally texted and told me that he was riding his scooter and came upon his best friend who was in an accident. He helped his friend get to the hospital, but his friend didn't make it. He seemed very upset and sad. He said his friend had a wife and two kids that needed his care, that she had no clue what to do and was relying on Chad to help.

He texted saying, "Thank you for understanding, I'm not blowing you off."

I felt so bad for him. I sent a "sorry for your loss" card to the hotel that he worked at since I had no other address for him and was hoping he would receive it.

A few days went by, then weeks with no word from Chad. I did not hear from him for the rest of the summer. I became so upset because the person that I was having a real connection with just stopped texting, as if he fell off the face of the earth. I wasn't getting through on his phone and was not receiving any replies. It really hurt. Then my mind went to thinking he was probably dating his friend's wife by now, and the hurt turned into anger. Eventually I decided to try to move on and forget about him.

I went about my summer and continued with my trail runs and surprisingly would get 1st and 2nd place in them (it helped being in an older age bracket). Having the support from my ex-boyfriend and my daughters meant so much. I finished the races with a 10K (6.2 miles), which was the furthest I have ever ran in my life. My youngest daughter even came to cheer me on and made a sign for me. I was so proud of myself to have accomplished all four runs and ending with the 10K. I even encouraged one of my other daughters and her friend to do a 5K cave run one month later, which was their first 5K. That run was amazing, running through the cave and experiencing it with my daughter. I was proud of her and her friend for attending and finishing, because even with my experience, that particular run was very hard.

I started trying to plan my future around Covid, hoping to get out of the medical field as a Respiratory Therapist and start a new career that didn't involve twelve-hour shifts and watching people die. It was getting harder and harder to work in a hospital. I would get attached to the patients and families and even would attend funerals. I was ready to move on; still work with people, just in a different way. I remembered that Chad and I had talked a lot about doing Airbnb together and how we would make a great team. That was super exciting, but now I was back to pursuing it on my own. My thoughts were that I could put in a six weeks' notice at my job in the fall and do the traveling Respiratory contracts to make the extra money to pursue my new dream. Plus, I wanted to be able to get a contract job out West to be near my family, even if it was only for thirteen weeks. This new idea seemed plausible, and I hated to constantly talk about something; I wanted to make it happen. So, to make it happen, I would have to quit my current job, be a traveling therapist for a couple years, then move to the beach and buy something to rent out. Maybe become a school bus driver or postal worker for the insurance, and maybe keep a part time job as a respiratory therapist. I could also be an events coordinator at a campground or mobile home park. I would like to inspire the older generation to get moving and enjoy life, maybe even be a motivator of some sort. My mind was racing of what my future might look like, but the only way to make it come true was to make it happen. As terrifying as it sounded, it seemed worth the try. Nobody ever dies from changing careers, right? That was that. My mind was made up, and when I make my mind up, that's it, there's no turning back.

Before I knew it, it was almost time for my road trip to Cookie's house for Labor Day weekend in September. Since I had been doing those trail runs, I was looking up what 5Ks would be available near her. I found one in Kissimmee that was on her day off, but I wasn't sure she would be up for it. It was a 5K naked run at a family-friendly nude resort. I asked her what she thought.

She said, "Hell yeah!"

With that, I signed us up! That is why I've always loved her: it was always a surprise as to what we would get ourselves into. The nude run was going to top everything we have ever done together and take our friendship somewhere else!

After arriving at her house, we laughed and giggled talking about the run. We agreed on sports bras for tops and as bottoms go, I wore a bikini bottom, and she wore a tutu.

Just before leaving her house, she says, "I don't think I can do this!"

"We signed up and we are going, we can do this!" I told her.

After a two hour drive and a few pep talks, we placed our sunglasses and hats on, then giggled quietly while waiting in line to register. We giggled for the first thirty minutes of arriving. They say it takes fifteen to forty-five minutes to acclimate yourself to that kind of environment. It was true; after a while our giggles subsided, and it didn't seem to affect us as much. Everyone was so nice, they treated you with respect, eyes never wandered, and everyone kept their boundaries. There were about one hundred thirty people in the run and most of them were men. I have never seen so much skin in one place in my life! It was an experience I'll never forget. I have a new outlook on nudists. I was impressed at how people were so comfortable in their skin, all shapes, and all sizes. They were people just like us, working people, businessmen and women who just wanted to feel the freedom of being naked. I have seen many bodies working in the hospital over the years, so it wasn't much different. It was just more of them in one place at one time. Everyone was enjoying the resort with its beautiful lake, pools, restaurant, gift shop, tennis courts, pickle ball courts, etc.

Cookie and I left after about an hour after the run and she said, "We just took our friendship to a whole new level!" I totally agreed.

We laughed all the way back to her house! As much fun as I was having, I couldn't stop thinking about Chad and how on that same day I had prior plans of driving on down to Key West to see him. I wondered what he was doing and who he was with. I did have a thought about just showing up at that resort where I met him at, but with my luck, he would be with someone, so I wasn't about to take that chance and be humiliated.

Fall was approaching and I decided to take another short trip home to see my family. I wanted to be there for one of my dad's surgeries, so I booked a ticket for October 6th to the 11th. I also decided to put my six weeks' notice in at work after I got back. The thought of not having a job lined up right away after my six weeks was finished was so nerve-wracking. The hospital I was working at had been my home hospital for almost ten years. I even helped open it up when it was brand new. I was hoping this trip to Seattle would help me to relax some and to give me clarity.

It was a great visit. My dad's surgery went well, and I was even able to go to a Seahawks game in Seattle with my brother. We had the best time even though we didn't get to see too much of the game since our seats were in the nosebleed section. Seattle can be a hit or miss with the weather that time of year too, but we lucked out with no rain, it was just a beautiful chilly West Coast night.

Prior to loading up my suitcase and saying my goodbyes, I noticed a missed phone call and text from long lost Chad. The text said that his phone was stolen, and he did not know my number or last name to find me until he opened his locker at work one day and found the card I sent. He said I put my phone number in it, and he sat on the floor to call me right away. I didn't have time to talk, so I sent back a reply saying I'd call him after I checked in at the airport. I had no idea what he was going to say, but I was anticipating the call.

After hugs and goodbyes were said with my parents, and I was all checked in at the airport, I had to find a spot to sit down and call Chad. It had been almost three months since we talked last.

I was a little nervous but also excited when I dialed his number. He answered right away. I told him I figured he had moved on with possibly his friend's family and kids, and maybe even married. He reassured me that he was not with her or anyone, that him and another friend were helping his dead friend's wife and the kids out as much as they could. After some time, however, they let her know she needed to go home to her family so her family could help and take over since she was abusing Chad and his friend's help. She started expecting them to babysit, etc. He said it was exhausting. He then said multiple times that he just knew I'd come walking around the corner one day to where we first met. Especially the weekend that I had said I was going down there and ended up staying with Cookie instead. I told him I wasn't going to make that trip to find out that he was with someone else and that he had moved on. I didn't need that slap in my face. I also said I knew that one day I'd hear from him again, I just knew. I told him that in the meantime I was pursuing my dreams and shared with him that I got my Florida Respiratory license, and I was about to put in my six weeks' notice at work. He was excited for me and kept saying I could work in Key West. Working in Key West sounded like fun, but I wasn't sure I wanted to be that far away from my kids.

Chad started asking if I was serious about the Airbnb and how we could build it together and make it happen, but only if I was willing and serious. I said I was, but I needed to get a job in Florida first to save some money and go from there. It made me happy to know someone was all about building a life together and supporting a dream of mine while adding their input and ideas. Could that really happen? We didn't talk too long since I had to board my plane. Talking to Chad lifted my spirits and gave me a lot to think about on my flight home.

I was back at work the next day and it was time to turn my notice in as planned. It was super hard.

That was a huge leap of faith, but I knew it was the right time for me. People didn't apply for traveling jobs until a few weeks out, so there were no guarantees. However, with COVID taking over, I knew the odds were in my favor.

All the stress and worry weighed on me and I ended up having heart palpitations that I could feel. I put on a heart monitor at work just to see what was happening and if anything would even show up. The machine told me what I had suspected: I was having PVC's (extra heart beats) that I noticed, and at one point my heart rate dropped to thirty-two! That is super low. It made me feel extremely tired. The cardiologist looked at my EKG and told me that it was not a life-threatening issue, and if I cut out coffee, exercise, and alcohol that I would be fine. Was she kidding me! I LOVED all three of those things. I would take my chances. Once I turned in my notice, I was feeling a little better. Stress can do some crazy things to your body. Over some time, everything seemed to feel normal again.

Chad and I talked regularly, and he kept asking me to come visit. He told me one of his buddies committed suicide and they found him on his own sailboat. His buddy's son named Sam drove down from up North to assess the boat. Sam told Chad he didn't want it. Chad said he bought the sailboat from Sam for $60,000. He explained that he would be moving onto it soon and wanted me to come down and stay on it with him. He added how we could fix it up and use it for Airbnb or even charter it out. He also said how we could get our captain's licenses and get paid a substantial sum of money to take people to islands and other countries. It would basically be a vacation for us, and we'd get to travel for free. It all sounded a little scary, but doable and exciting.

I checked my schedule, and I had a weekend off at the end of October, which was during the Key West Fantasy Fest, and a perfect time to go visit. To be able to be in Key West during Fantasy Fest and to stay on a sailboat at the same time. That all sounded wonderful and intriguing. I booked my plane ticket and started looking for costumes for both Fantasy Fest and Halloween. We were both thrilled to be able to finally be together after texting, calling, and Face Timing each other for weeks. October 29th couldn't arrive soon enough. I was walking around with a smile on my face daily. Could all this really be happening? Could you really have a connection with someone in that short amount of time? Did I keep my guard up or did I go for it? My heart was telling me to go for it, but my gut was a little hesitant. I needed to be with him over a weekend to really find out for sure. I packed my carry-on, and I was ready for my weekend getaway with Chad.

Chapter 3

(Fantasy Fest)

After landing in Key West, I had to wait a few minutes for Chad to pick me up on his scooter. I was looking cute wearing a sexy summer top, my holey jeans, wedges, sunglasses, and a hat on. I realized nobody wears much but flip flops and sandals on an island, but the wedges went along with one of my costumes and I needed to save space in my carry-on. As soon as he pulled up, he walked up to me and gave me a big hug and kiss. He looked so good with his tan skin and beautiful hazel eyes that were just as mesmerizing as I remembered. My wedges made me taller which made him look down at my shoes, then he looked back at me and just smiled. He said he had been waiting for me to come back to him since we first met in July. And then said he couldn't wait for me to see his new sailboat, that with a little work here and there, we could make it shine like a champ.

Chad had to arrange for someone to follow us to haul my suitcase in their truck to the docks since he didn't think it would fit on the scooter with both of us. Here I was, in Key West riding on the back of a scooter with a local on our way to the docks, wearing wedges. It seemed silly but I didn't care, I was enjoying every second. The smell of the ocean and the warm wind blowing through my hair felt stimulating. Chad paid the guy for helping us with my suitcase and then was looking for David, the person who would be towing Chad's dinghy to take us to Chad's new boat. A dinghy is a much smaller boat

31

usually towed behind a bigger boat. It's an easier way to navigate around than on the bigger boat, especially if the bigger boat was a sailboat or yacht that was too big for the docks. Dinghies can range from an inflatable raft to a simple wooden boat. Chad mentioned the engine of his dinghy was not working properly, so it had to be towed. A boat came around the corner with Chad's inflatable dinghy being towed behind it. I climbed aboard that dinghy with my suitcase and a couple of Chad's suitcases since he was moving onto the boat permanently. Chad was going to ride with David who was towing the dinghy. I noticed how people were looking at me, probably wondering who I was, assuming that I was a city girl. It didn't really bother me, I was enjoying myself, they didn't know me.

Chad's sailboat was on a mooring ball out in the water, so a dinghy is very important: it's your transportation between home and land. When we all got situated and set off, I felt great! I was living life to the fullest with the sun on my skin, wind in my hair, and ocean water on my face, all the while being towed on a dinghy to his sailboat. I was with a guy that seemed to be truly interested in me, who wanted the same things I did, and we were going to make it happen! There was no other place I'd rather be, it all felt perfect. I noticed the winds were picking up and the water was getting very choppy, but the cool, salt water, hitting my face felt refreshing. When we were in close proximity, I recognized the sailboat from a picture Chad had sent me: it was a good-sized sailboat, a forty-two foot Endeavor. It was older but had a good body and I could envision her shine with some TLC like Chad said.

Earlier, Chad had explained to me that since he just bought the boat, all the stuff on it was from the previous owner, his best friend. Therefore, I was somewhat prepared before stepping onto the sailboat. The driver tied off the dinghy and helped me aboard my potential new home on the water. Chad said we would get our suitcases later because he needed to get ready to go into work for a while. He wanted to make sure I was going to be okay out on the boat all alone. I had snacks and some water and said I would be fine. He felt bad to leave me alone, but he had no choice (RED FLAG), they needed him at the hotel since it was Fantasy Fest, and they were short on workers. The hotel was fully booked. I totally understood and I was just happy to be in Key West on a boat. I was kind-of hoping we would have been able to enjoy some of the festivities that night, but there was always the next night.

Chad left with David after we said goodbye and it was then that I was all alone on a sailboat. A sailboat I had never been on before. I didn't even know how to drive a boat. Is that what it's even called, driving? Also, what was I going to do for the next several hours by myself? He did say that he had a buddy he was paying to give us rides back and forth while I was there in town, and to call him if I needed anything. I didn't want to bother anyone, so I decided to stay put and enjoy the sun before it would eventually set. It was peaceful and the water was so blue. I decided to venture inside to take a closer look

33

around. It was messy and had a musty smell, but I was willing to overlook the mess since a single man lived on it. I opened a couple windows to help with the smell. I had to use the bathroom; there were 2, so I picked one. When I opened the door, the smell was overwhelmingly awful, and there was no running water. I should have had Chad show me how to use the bathroom correctly so I wouldn't mess anything up. I tried the other bathroom, and it was the same. The toilets looked like they had never been cleaned before, along with the kitchen. I had to search for the toilet paper and figure out how to use the pump on the toilet. While working on that, I thought what the hell was I doing? I should be staying in a hotel with a clean bathroom and running water! But there I was in Key West, with a fantastic guy that wanted to help me make my dreams a reality. I tried staying positive so I looked around the boat and observed how it could be turned into a nice little house, and I do mean little! There was definite potential. Living on a boat would be a whole different lifestyle, one that was fascinating to me. That would be my next adventure! I went back up on the deck to watch the sunset (and to not have to smell the odor from the bathroom). I had brought a small bottle of rum, and I was wanting to make myself a drink, but with the rocking of the boat, I thought I'd better not. I did not want to get seasick with no running water. I decided I would stick with my soda.

The sunset over the water that night was beautiful, and I felt at peace as the sky went dark. After watching the sunset, I was really wanting my suitcase for a change of clothes, but it was still out on the dinghy. How hard would it be to climb down and get it? I tried to climb down the backside of the sailboat (also known as the stern) on a ladder. The seas seemed to know what I was up to and decided to make it more challenging for me. Suddenly, the winds picked up and rocked the boat more and more as I decided to go for my suitcase. As I had one leg on the sailboat and one leg on the dinghy, the water was splashing up on me with each wave. The sailboat was rocking opposite of the dinghy which felt like I was riding the waves with my legs. I was using every muscles in my legs to not slip and fall in the water. There was too much space in between the boat and the dinghy that in an instant I would be overboard and in the ocean. I'm not one that could ever do the splits and I was not about to start now, but if I didn't go one way or the other, I was about to find out what the splits felt like. My whole body started shaking and I got a little scared looking into the ocean not knowing what could be under that dark surface. My fight or flight mode kicked in and I needed to do something soon. If I didn't hurry, I was going to not only find out what lies beneath, but also what the water temperature was. The waves and the winds were making it quite treacherous. Even if I did make it on the dinghy, how was I going to get my suitcase back over the water and up the ladder? I didn't want to get stuck on the dinghy as high as the swells were getting. I decided to hold on to the boat with everything I had and pull my shaking leg up and over the ladder and climb back aboard. After climbing aboard, I sat down and let out a big sigh. I tried but no success. I was safe and mostly dry, so I decided to remain positive. I could brush my teeth the next day, and the clothes I had on were comfy enough to sleep in.

It was getting late, so I decided to go to bed. Chad had fixed one of the bedrooms up with clean sheets, blankets, and pillows. It wasn't bad and with the energy I just used up, and the rocking of the boat, I fell asleep quite easily.

Not once did I think of anything bad that could have happened or how dangerous it might have been to be out on a sailboat by myself. Only a few people knew where I was: Chad, David, his friend who he was paying to take us back and forth to land, and whomever else Chad may have told. My friends from work knew I was in Key West, but nobody knew what boat I was on. The boat was out in the ocean surrounded by other boats, and some of them looked the same. I put my trust in Chad and felt safe. I look back now and think about how lucky I am to be writing this book. How dangerous that was, for a woman to be taken out to a boat and left by herself. Anything could have happened. I am too trustworthy and adventurous at times. I never even thought about the "what ifs or RED FLAGS."

I didn't hear a boat come up, only Chad walking down into the bedroom sometime after midnight. He apologized again for having to work. Even though he was exhausted, we stayed up talking and cuddling for a couple hours before falling asleep.

The next morning, we sat on the deck of the boat watching the sunrise. With the multiple colors of oranges and reds, I thought this view could never get old. It was so beautiful and serene. Chad was smoking a cigarette and told me he planned on quitting, mainly for me since he knew I was a respiratory therapist. He said he would change anything for me. I stared into his eyes wondering how he could be serious; we haven't known each other that long. Can people really fall for each other this quick? I didn't say too much back, I just smiled, taking it all in.

He decided it was time to retrieve the suitcases from the dinghy. I stayed on the sailboat to help bring them aboard. The swells were not as big as the night before, but still bad enough that Chad almost lost his footing a couple times. We transferred them aboard and since it was Fantasy Fest and Halloween, I had packed a couple of outfits for both of us. Chad was excited and ready to see what I packed for us. He didn't seem to mind anything that I brought up or ideas I had, he just went along with them. That hasn't been my experience with dating, and it was a nice change of pace. He was making it even more exciting.

His friend came to take us to shore for the day. After being dropped off at the docks, Chad took me to his favorite place for breakfast called Harpoon Harry's which was close by. It was delicious. We had fun sitting outside eating while watching the diversity of people walking by. Since it was Fantasy Fest, there were outfits of all kinds, even costumes that were just painted on the naked body. I met some of Chad's friends and the locals that he helped. Chad would even pay a local to watch his bicycle for him so nobody would mess with it or steal it. He said he tried to help the locals as much as he could. I saw him give his friend $200.00 to take us back and forth to his boat and the guy said that since gas prices were up that he was going to need $100.00 more, so Chad gave it to him. I was thinking these people were totally take advantage of Chad since he had money. It didn't seem to bother him, if he even knew.

We walked around while he was telling me about this place and that place and even introduced me to some more people he knew. Chad was pleased to have me there and said everyone would be surprised to see him with someone since he is usually alone. Chad worked six days a week, so he didn't have time to date. We had a great time enjoying the town and each other. While in town, I asked if we could stop at Kermit's to find out what happened to the key lime pie that he said he sent to my parents that past July. Chad said of course and that we could do that the next day. I didn't think about asking to check on it right then, and never wondered why he didn't just say yes immediately. (RED FLAG)

Chad wanted to introduce me to this couple he knew sitting on one of the benches at the docks with their young boy. After the introductions, the couple apologized for their son being so sad and unfriendly. They said someone just stole his bike. Chad instantly was on the child's level and told him that he would give him his own bike. The boy perked up and was instantly happy. Chad said he would get his bike serviced and then let the boy have it in a few days. He said he didn't need it and that was the least he could

38

do. The couple was very appreciative, and the boy was ecstatic. I was honored to be standing next to this gentleman who was so very generous. He seemed to be so genuine about helping others and putting them above himself. That was the way life should be, everyone helping each other. We are all on this planet together trying to make it. A little kindness goes a long way.

We left the now happy family and were waiting for our ride back out to his boat when we ran into one of his almost homeless friends named Jerry. Jerry lived on a tiny boat next to Chad. Jerry's boat didn't even have any shade on it, and I wasn't really sure how it was considered livable. I was introduced to Jerry, and he was pleased to meet me. Jerry asked Chad if his little boat was looking any better. Jerry said he saved up all of his money to purchase a can of paint to fix it up. He earned his money by sweeping for a local business. Chad told him it was looking great and that he was doing an amazing job. Jerry said thank you with the biggest grin on his face. He was so proud of himself.

Jerry then looked at me and said, "Nice meeting you Niki Rae."

"It was a pleasure meeting you too, Jerry," I replied.

After getting back to the boat, we had a couple of hours to hang out before getting ready to go back into town for the evening, so we sat on the deck talking. Chad told me about his Ranger school for the

Army. He said that right there in Key West, during training, they would drop you off in the ocean and you had to swim to shore. Chad continued talking about being a Ranger and how he worked his way up to a First Sergeant. He said he oversaw over one hundred men and told me how he went overseas on multiple tours. The tours were hard to speak about because too many bad things happened in front of him, making him have nightmares still. He then changed the subject and talked about why he didn't drink or do drugs. His parents were greatly affected and after watching what they went through, he decided that he was not going to be a part of that. However, Chad mentioned he did have a medical marijuana card, for the back pains he had from his tours from being a Ranger. He explained that he only took that when he was in pain, just to relax him. He also talked about how he was tossed back and forth from his mom to his stepdad and explained that his stepdad was in the Mafia in New Jersey (RED FLAG). Eventually he was raised by his Italian family and for punishment his grandma would make him copy the New Testament, and even the dictionary. That explains how he knew so many lesser-known words. He spoke five languages: English, Spanish, German, Italian, and Russian. I heard him speak Spanish and Italian on occasion. All throughout his story, I sat and listened, trying to process it all. There were a lot of things he went through that I had not had to deal with growing up, and as he was talking about it, I felt bad for him and his rough childhood. I couldn't imagine living like he did. Later I recognize that he did most of the talking again.

40

We were looking out at a boat pulling a parasail and Chad mentioned that he wanted to live life and do adventures like that, not be in the bars every night. He said he didn't want to just exist. That made me smile because that's exactly how I wanted to live. Could I have found the one person who wanted the same things as I did in this life?

As relaxing as it was on the boat, it was time for our ride into town and to experience Fantasy Fest. I had brought a policewoman outfit for that first night for me. The next night I had a 70's outfit for both Chad and I. As skimpy as the policewoman outfit seemed to me, I was still overdressed compared to most. Chad didn't have an outfit and he felt out of place wishing he had something to wear. We stopped in a few tourist shops thinking we would find something for him, but no such luck. We found the webcam outside of Sloppy Joe's and waved to my friends at work who knew I was in Key West. It was so entertaining watching everyone and all the fantastic costumes, I had never seen anything like it.

Everywhere we went, Chad would buy me and whomever we were talking to whatever drinks we liked. He was a perfect gentleman, always watching out for me. We had a wonderful time listening to great music, enjoying each other and of course people watching. At one time we were on a balcony of a bar across the street from Sloppy Joe's looking down at the crowd of people and enjoying all the costumes. I noticed the military men on top of Sloppy Joe's, and I said something to Chad about them guarding the place. He went along with me for a minute.

41

Then he said, "Those are Sloppy Joe's bartenders dressed up, it IS Fantasy Fest after all!"

I was so embarrassed about thinking they were real. They really did look the part. He teased me about that many times over. We laughed and laughed over again about it. He said that would be a story told many times to come.

We spotted a group of prisoners in costume, and since I was a policewoman, they let me take a picture with them. Everyone was having such a good time. Fantasy Fest was something you had to experience for yourself to understand. It was one of those things that was hard to explain.

It was getting late, and we had to catch a ride out to the boat for the night, even though Key West was alive and kicking. It was an exciting day and night, and I was ready to settle down for a good night's sleep. The rocking of the ocean was like being in a baby's cradle, it was so relaxing and soothing that it really did put you to sleep.

The next morning, we sat on the deck, sipping our coffee and enjoying another beautiful sunrise while listening to the quiet of the ocean. There was no need to speak when you were taking in Mother Nature. It was nice to be able to spend quiet time with someone and not feel awkward about it. It seemed like we sat in silence for hours, when, in reality, it was only about thirty minutes. In that moment of quietness, Chad asked if I was with anyone when he lost his phone, and we weren't speaking for almost three months. For a relationship to work, you must be honest and open. I told him that I had a dinner date with someone. That's all that it was, and I thought about Chad the whole time wishing it was him. I told him all of that. He just listened. I asked him the same question and he answered with he's never laid eyes on anyone since we met. His eyes seemed to tell the truth. I only heard stories like that in the movies. Can I really believe that was happening to me? Only time will tell, I imagined.

It was time to get our backpacks and get a ride to shore. I packed some personal items since he said I could use the marina showers after he got a key from one of the ladies he worked with at the hotel. Her husband was the one Chad was paying to transport us from Chad's boat to shore and back. He said he got her the job at the hotel, and she wouldn't mind me using her bathroom card. I never knew when I would get to use the showers, so I packed my personal stuff with me at all times in my backpack. Sometimes it seemed like chaos correlating times to get a ride and getting the shower key from his friends. I knew we were on island time, and nobody was in any kind of hurry, but good grief. A shower always felt great whenever I did get one.

After brunch I wanted to watch some of the Seahawks' game, so Chad took me to a local sports bar. Later we played some pool and darts. Then it was time to change into our costumes for Halloween. He was eager to participate, and I loved that. We each had a wig, and if I didn't have a blonde wig, we would have look like Sonny and Cher. We took off on his scooter and cruised Duval Street with people waving, honking, and whistling at us. It was as if we were movie stars. When we parked and walked around, people stopped us to take our picture. It was so enjoyable. We stopped in at Sloppy Joe's to do some dancing and I had no idea how good of a dancer Chad was!

I could have stayed out all night dancing with him, but we had to keep watching the time since the only ride we had back to the boat was at 10pm. Any later and we would be staying on the island. We felt like two teenagers having so much fun and having a curfew. The curfew part was upsetting. I know we would have won the costume contest that night if we stayed, because we looked so good. He said we could make that a thing: we could dress up like that once a week and go to a local bar to do karaoke and sing Sonny and Cher's song "I Got You Babe" and then walk out. The same time each week. I loved that idea and loved that I was with someone who thought like me. I would totally do that.

"Do you want to people watch or be watched by people?" Chad said.

I enjoy people watching, but there's something about being in costume and pretending to be someone you're not with everyone watching you. It sounded like so much fun. He added that we could take ballroom dance classes to get better and learn a choreographed dance. We could go out on the dance floor and act like we didn't know much about dancing and then break out in a planned couples dance. I think he watched a lot of YouTube and TikTok clips. I didn't mind because all of that sounded awesome to me. It also seemed like a great way to stay fun and young. I was all in.

After dancing as long as we could, we made it to his friends at the docks before our curfew time was up. His friends were in some kind of mood. Too many drinks? Not sure, but we were ready for our ride. I was wondering why we didn't just stay at the hotel he worked at. I figured he probably wanted to be on his new boat since he just bought it, so I didn't question it.

After climbing aboard Chad's boat, we changed into more comfortable clothes and was reminiscing over the evening and laughed about all the different costumes we encountered and how everyone loved ours. Our costumes were a big hit.

I loved how we connected, and we were both affectionate and loved touching each other, he was so gentle. It was as if we had known each other forever, it felt so comfortable. I would melt when he would kiss me on the forehead. From the forehead, it would be kisses on the neck which made me tingle and come alive. He knew how to kiss and how to touch and where to touch, a pleaser. He seemed to know women. We broke in the boat that night. Being able to have all the windows open with the breeze blowing through while making love was stimulating. The smallness of the boat came in handy to be able to grab walls, ceilings, bookcases, etc. when needed. We were exploring each other over and over and over again, and it was intoxicating. Needless to say, we slept like babies that night.

It was my last full day in Key West and Chad had to be the pool guy at the hotel that day. He said I could get in and hang out with him after about two hours from his start time. I had my backpack and grabbed some coffee and hung out at the docks while waiting. I was looking forward to laying out by a pool for the day. My equilibrium was a little off that morning since I kept feeling the rocking of the ocean while walking on land. I was guessing that was something you got used to.

I found my spot next to the pool for the day overlooking the ocean. It was another beautiful day along with some amazing scenery. Chad was literally the pool guy handing people towels and controlling the music.

As more people gathered around the pool, I was able to witness how Chad interacted with everyone. The tourists loved him. He was very personal, witty, and funny. He had everyone laughing and enjoying his company. One of the girls even took his picture because she said he looked like one of the guys in the show Yellowstone. She invited him to join their party that evening. He just smiled at them and said maybe next time. He brought me some lunch from a local sandwich shop and bought me a drink from the pool bar. I was enjoying being pampered while laying by the pool with the ocean as my backdrop.

I decided to get in the hot tub and a couple men about my age joined me on the opposite side. It was big and there was plenty of room. We started small talk, because why not, and I'm all about making new friends wherever I go. I noticed Chad looking my way being very watchful. After a while of conversing and getting warmed up from the hot water, I got out and sat next to Chad. He instantly asked me what they wanted and what we were talking about (RED FLAG). I wasn't sure how to take that because that's how I always act when I meet new people, I was social. It did feel somewhat good to have someone care about my wellbeing and be slightly jealous.

In the middle of the day during Chad's shift, he ran out for about ten minutes. When he came back, he told me he just sold his BMW for almost pennies to his friend who needed a car. He said he didn't need it. I never did see the car, unless it was the same one I saw on the YouTube channel when he was talking about Hurricane Irma. I was a little confused at why someone would do that since you may need a car one day, but it wasn't any of my business. I shrugged off my thoughts and kept them to myself.

His shift was up, and we were about to leave when he got involved in a conversation with a group of tourists. They were thanking Chad for being a great host and was leaving him a box of alcohol that they were unable to take on their flight home. They saw me standing there and asked Chad if I was his wife.

He turned to me smiling and said, "Maybe soon."

I blushed and smiled back. He told me that he gets people giving him stuff all the time that they cannot take with them on their plane ride home. He doesn't drink so he'd give it all away to the people living on the homeless island, which I thought was sweet and caring.

That afternoon Chad was talking to a coworker to try and get her to cover his shift the following day so he could take me to the airport. She was not having it. He said he tried talking to his boss to have a couple hours off, but that wasn't working either. Chad was getting nervous about it and said he may just go in and quit the job. They have been working him like a dog lately with very little time off. He said he didn't need it anyway, that he only took the job to keep himself from being bored. In fact, he never even cashed any of their checks; he just placed them in a drawer (RED FLAG). He said he had enough money coming in from rental property that he had in New Jersey.

On the walk to the docks, we stopped to have dinner at a local restaurant. One of the locals that I met the day before was walking by and she remembered me and stopped to say hi. She told me I was welcome back anytime, that we had a connection. I felt as though she was sincere and accepted me. That made me feel welcomed.

While on the ride back to the boat Chad told me that one of the neighbors said they heard us talking the other night.

I said, "Oh?"

Then I realized what he meant. It didn't register how much sound travels over the water with no barriers in between all the boats. Oops, my bad. Not that I'm apologizing for making any noises. We laughed about it. I would be more cautious of that the next time around.

The evening went well, and we watched the sunset one last time. I was already sad to be leaving so soon, since it had been a wonderful weekend. I tried being a little quieter that night and later we held each other a little tighter knowing I was leaving the next day.

While having our coffee the next morning on the deck, Chad was telling me he would do whatever I needed him to do. He was already going to quit smoking, but he added he would shave or wax his chest if that was what I wanted. Whatever it takes, he said (RED FLAG). I answered by telling him he was fine and that he didn't need to change anything.

He was telling me he would have the bathrooms all cleaned up by the next time I came to see him, and how he planned on gutting the kitchen and making it ours, with a granite countertop and a new stove and refrigerator. All of that sounded great. I was looking forward to seeing the renovation of the place.

Mid-morning Chad decided he was going into town to quit his job. Then he would come back to take me to the airport. I wasn't really sure he was going to quit his job until he came back all rejuvenated telling me how he went about it. He was definitely not going to get rehired there after the way he quit. He said he did all that for me (RED FLAG). Well, if he didn't need the money, then that wasn't that big of a loss, I supposed, except he seemed to love people and enjoyed working at that hotel around all the tourists. I'm sure there was another hotel he could work at if needed. He said that would give him more time to fix up the boat for us and our future. I liked the thought of that.

We were in a rush to get me to the airport, and I was a little disappointed that we didn't have time to stop at Kermit's to see what happened with the key lime pie. I really wanted my parents to receive a key lime pie from Chad, to show them what a great guy he was.

My suitcase fit in-between us on his scooter this time, so off to the airport we went.

He asked if I was leaving satisfied and I said, "Of course I am, I will be leaving with a smile on my face!"

That made him happy. We hugged a long, tight hug and he kept asking me to just stay there with him on "our" boat. I said I had to go, even though I wanted to stay. Then he kissed me on the forehead and looked me long in the eyes and finally said, "Then hurry back to me, I'll be waiting." We parted ways on a bittersweet note: sad I was leaving but hopeful we would see each other again real soon.

I have never had anyone want me as bad as he did. It made me feel special. It was hard to believe. I have been such a giver in past relationships, so it was refreshing to be with someone who was giving up so much already just for me. Planning a business together and building off my dreams to make them bigger than I could even imagine, was the highlight for me, but it really was a lot to think about.

I was still a little skeptical, but it was getting easier to let that fade as I was falling for everything Chad was saying to me. He was the person that was made for me: Someone who wanted to build a future together, a partner, someone who loves people, loves living life to the fullest. He was cute, tall, could dance, had a sense of humor, spontaneous, and a hard worker. Money didn't seem to be an issue, and he would do anything for me; he says he can cook and loves kids and animals. It was looking so good and promising, and I was also starting to feel connected to Key West. It seemed the more I was around Chad and the more we talked, the more I liked, even though it was a lot to absorb.

They say that you meet "the one" when you're not looking, and I certainly was not looking, I was having fun with my friend Cookie when I met Chad. So maybe that was true. Could he be the one? Could this really happen to me? Why not? It happens to other people, so why not me? Those were questions that were going through my mind.

It was time to redirect and focus on my last days of work and finding a new job.

Sadly, it was goodbye to Chad and Key West, but hopefully for not too long.

Chapter 4

(Downsizing)

It was now early November and Chad and I had been texting back and forth since I left him in Key West. The first day back at work I became busy with my patients, and I figured Chad was also busy since I didn't hear from him for a few hours. I didn't think anything about it.

He then messaged me saying, "Since you didn't hear from me right away, you are probably with that guy you said you had dinner with when I lost my phone, and so I don't think this is going to work." (Red flag).

I was taken aback when I read that. Where did that come from? Why is he sending me that? I thought he trusted me. Before I could set him straight, he blocked me, and that was the last I heard from him for a few weeks. He ghosted me. I started thinking I should have never told him I went to dinner with someone, but he asked, and I was honest. I didn't think dinner with someone was that big of a deal. Especially since we weren't talking at that time. He obviously had some trust issues.

I was telling my friend Sarah at work about his message, and she was telling me to let him be, that he was a phony and that something wasn't right about him. She had been saying that since I met him. I didn't see it that way; I saw this person that was charming and exciting.

As absurd as that text was, I decided to focus on my plans, which included a volunteer trip to Costa Rica in a few days for a week that I was extremely looking forward to. Another solo trip, except when I arrived, I would be with a group of people, so really only solo at the airports. We were all going there to volunteer with the sloths.

I had an amazing week in Costa Rica and met some wonderful people. It was a great way to decompress from worrying about my future, a job, and Chad, even though all three of those crossed my mind quite often during my trip. Traveling to different destinations on the island and working with the sloths were truly astounding. I was finally getting out of my comfort zone and trying new things. We watched the monkeys playing in the trees, helped at an animal rescue park, hiked the Amazon, and even did some white-water rafting. I met a few lifelong friends, and we were all talking about where we would all meet up next time before saying our goodbyes. They told me to forget about Chad and to move on with my life. I told them that I was trying.

While I was unpacking from my trip, I received a job offer at a hospital in Gainesville, Florida. I had worked at that same hospital twenty years prior and decided to accept a twenty-six-week contract there starting in January. Everything was falling into place. I found an Airbnb room with a shared living space and bathroom, and within walking distance of the hospital. I only had three days left of work at my current job, so the timing was perfect. Those six weeks went by faster than I thought. It was sad to be leaving a place I called home, but I was also excited for this new turn in my life. I had all the holidays off with no work for the first time in years. A new chapter was developing, and I felt sure about my future even as frightening as it seemed.

Thanksgiving came and I decided to text Chad and tell him Happy Thanksgiving, not even sure if he would get it or not since he blocked me. To my surprise, he texted back immediately. He told me thank you, and that he'd been lying face down crying like a baby since he recently found out his grandma died. He seemed very upset, so I called him, and we chatted for quite a while. It was as if we had never stopped talking. We fell back in the routine of texting on a regular basis. We started FaceTiming each other more often. I even took him out to a restaurant with me! I propped my phone up against the napkin holder and while he was eating at Harpoon Harry's in Key West, Florida, I was eating sushi at my favorite Japanese restaurant in Madison, Alabama. It felt like we were falling back in love with the way we related to one another, and before I knew it, he asked me if I was all in.

I said, "Yes," even though I was starting a new job and chapter in my life.

Both of our spirits were up and excited to be on the same page again. Life was good.

There were times where I wouldn't hear from him for a couple days and I'd start to get a little concerned that he was getting cold feet again, or whatever that was before. One example was when I got a new phone and he let me know that I had silenced my notifications. I had no idea I did that or even how to do that. After that message I didn't hear from him for two days. My mind was thinking that he was probably suspicious and thinking I silenced them because I was seeing someone. The only person I was seeing was my grandson and kids. I started asking him what was wrong and if something happened because I was getting worried. He finally texted back saying he was sea-trialing the sailboat and that he was in and out of reception. I apologized for jumping to conclusions, but that he needed to let me know next time so I wouldn't worry.

I would send him a picture here and there of outfits I was wearing for that day, and he would always say, "Still Beautiful," or "You make anything look amazing." If I finished an art piece, I would send him a picture right away and get compliments from him. I had just finished a wood piece that the manager of the local Twin Peaks purchased to hang in their restaurant and Chad was very proud of it.

It was quite often he would go hours or days without texting back. Usually his phone wasn't charged, or he dropped it in the ocean, dropped it on the sidewalk, or had it in rice, or accidentally left it at Harpoon Harry's (Red flag). He admitted how clumsy he was and how he was always losing his phone, and that I'd find that out soon enough. He added that I would become the keeper of his phone then. Another reason I wouldn't hear from him was because he was always busy with working on the sailboat, the dinghy, or helping someone else out. He had told me one of the guys I met told him to tell me hi and to hurry back, that they all missed me. I thought how nice, and I was thrilled that they liked me.

It was getting close to Christmas and Chad had mentioned he may fly up to see me. Of course, I was wanting to make plans for us right away. He had told me about a job he had based out of Fort Lauderdale where he was in charge of trucks delivering clean waste to restaurants that was better for the environment. Flying up there would give him an opportunity to talk to them about his schedule. He said he probably would have to work through the holidays since he wasn't married nor had any kids, but that he would let me know.

Chad was getting restless and tired of helping his friends. He just wanted to get the sailboat ready for us to charter out. I'm not sure when he was wanting to do all that, because I signed a twenty-six week contract, so I would not be available until that was completed. He talked a lot about starting this and starting that and what we could do, etc. He reminded me of myself, having random ideas that came into my mind and things I'd like to do. I started wondering what it would be like living with someone that thought like me. I wasn't sure if that would be a good thing or a bad thing, but it sounded exciting.

Another idea Chad came up with was sailing up the coast to be closer to me, to "breathe me in." He wanted us to be together every day. I thought that would be awesome, but the closest marina to Gainesville was an hour to an hour and a half away. I was thinking that it wouldn't be too bad to drive that far to work for three days a week. So, we decided to do some research to see if that was a real possibility.

A few days before Christmas he tells me a story about when he was coming back from going to the store. He texted:

"I noticed three drunk guys kissing all over a drunk woman. I assisted the woman and handled the situation accordingly, so to speak. I got arrested as well as the three guys. I got released and no charges because I was assisting the woman. I have zero bruises or scratches. The cops asked me how come I'm not scratched or beat up as they were taking pictures of my hands. The officer at the desk said, 'Those guys were lucky. It says right here (as he pointed to his computer screen), he is a retired E-8 Army Ranger. That's why he isn't bruised up like them.' Lol. I honestly just stood there and raised an eyebrow and shrugged at the officers, taking pics of my hands. Five hours later they release me with zero charges. Free to go. Nada. All I did was help. They also advised me to be careful with my hands as I could be charged different than a civilian would. I understood." (RED FLAG)

It sounded like a crazy story, but then again it was Key West and crazy stuff like that did happen. I told him I was glad he was okay and didn't get hurt. He said he would always help women, children, handicapped, and the elderly. I told him that made me feel good and thankful that I would always be protected when we went out, and to be with someone that truly cared about others.

It was Christmas Eve and I sent him a couple pictures of myself wearing a cute sexy Christmas outfit. The sadness hit me after not hearing from him for a couple hours. A girl wants to hear how sexy she looks when she sends her man some pictures. Especially since there was thought, and time involved. Plus, it was Christmas Eve. A text finally came through a few hours later telling me how amazing I looked. Apparently, he had been out collecting clams for his dinner since it was low tide. He also said he was going diving on Christmas Day for lobster to go with the clams, so he wouldn't be able to talk since he would be underwater (RED FLAG). That was not what I wanted to hear. Although, fresh lobster sounded delightful, and I couldn't wait to be able to enjoy that with him one day. He kept mentioning what a good cook he was and that one day soon I would find out. We FaceTimed each other that night and talked about seafood and living on a boat together.

A few days went by, and I mentioned I was feeling a little sad not hearing from him, mostly because it was Christmas. I've always felt that Christmas was a time to be with and spend time with the ones you love. He replied:

"Good morning sweetheart. Don't feel sad, I apologize for not being on point. Yesterday I went diving for a bit. Free diving for lobsters. Today I'm up to my elbows in grease in the engine room. Greasing up parts of the engine getting her ready for transport.

Just doing boat stuff hun. There is a lot to this life. A lot of checking and rechecking. You will see. I'm doing all of this so we can be."

I told him I was pleased to hear that because I wanted us to be too.

The next day he was going to open up the sheets (sails) to air them out, start the engine, and do a systems check. He then tells me that so far all of that has hit him for 11K (RED FLAG) to get the sailboat ready for overseas travel. He said he just needed to get to the mooring and to fish and to see me.

I was getting excited about starting my new job and seeing him again, so I showed him a picture of all my bins full of clothes that I was taking with me to Gainesville and possibly be moving them onto the boat if we got a marina.

He said, "Ummm. Not all of that is going to fit on the boat hun."

Realizing he was probably right, I decided to go through more of my stuff and do some downsizing. I was getting hot flashes wearing some of my sweaters, so those needed to go. There was not going to be a need for some of my boots and high heeled shoes either. I ended up having a few large boxes of clothes that I gave away. Some new boat clothes would be on my list of things I needed once in Florida.

After sharing a lot of my art with him, Chad started telling me I had a talent with my woodwork

60

and how inspired he was, that I could set up a business on my laptop. He said we could take our bikes out exploring and pick up antique finds that would be worth selling and making a profit online also. His mind did not stop turning on how to make money.

He texted later saying, "Mangrove root is worth a good penny. I have about three million in stock of that (RED FLAG). I have Wisteria/Christmas tree island. It's full of it, lol."

Most of his days were being used up by helping his friends. He was worn-out from trying to help a friend get his mom out of jail and her boat out of impound (Another "heroic" event) (RED FLAG). He said he would be better when he stopped helping and supporting everyone, that it would be nice if someone would just order him a pizza, that it was very draining. I couldn't help but wonder why he was just then coming to that conclusion. I didn't say anything though.

New Year's Eve came, and we talked about how we couldn't wait for 2022. It was going to be the year we got our love story officially started, to be wrapped up into each other. We were going to have so many adventures together! We decided to do a YouTube channel of our experiences and adventures on the boat. He was going to video his side of getting the boat ready and the journey of sailing it up, and I was going to video my side waiting for him and finding us a marina. Then we would join together and video our life on the boat. I ordered myself a GoPro to start the documenting on my side and I was waiting for its arrival. Every day I could hardly contain my excitement.

A big snow landed a couple days into January, after a few days of sun. That's how Alabama weather is, it could be seventy-eight degrees one day and snowing the next. It was the good kind of snow: perfect for making snowmen. I sent Chad a picture of me all bundled up out in the snow and of a small snowman I made.

"Still beautiful. Aren't you going to be glad to rid yourself of snow for a while?" he said.

I definitely was looking forward to the warmer weather, even though I enjoyed the snow from time to time, especially during the holidays. I didn't mention anything about the snow, but I did ask him if he was going to say that I'm still beautiful when I was eighty years old.

"Even at ninety and I will iron out those wrinkles for you every day if I have to," he said. I was swooning all over again.

Chapter 5

(Florida)

It was January 7th, and time for my road trip to Florida and to move into my room. My truck was loaded down with everything I might possibly need for twenty-six weeks. I felt like I was moving my daughter into a new dorm room or an apartment, which happened every year while she was in college. I had to chuckle because it was me moving myself this time, but without any help. Even though I wasn't going to college, the hospital I was going to work at was on the campus of the University of Florida, so I really did feel like a college kid. I even had to get my own parking pass. It was definitely a college town, with kids zipping around everywhere on their scooters, bicycles, and skateboards, all with their backpacks or binders. My new place was small but efficient. It was a shared kitchen and living area and my room had a bed, a desk, and a closet. My roommate was a young girl in her twenties from India on an anesthesia assistant rotation at the hospital. Luckily, we got along well, mainly because we rarely crossed paths. After getting all settled in, I had a few days to kill before starting my new job, so I made the choice to drive on down to see Cookie for a night.

I was telling Cookie and her guy all about Chad and our plans and showed them a picture of his sailboat. She was a little skeptical, so I convinced Chad to join us on FaceTime. I wanted her to see what a great guy he was. It was nice having Chad there with us, but I could tell he was getting a little jealous. Not sure why since I wasn't doing anything wrong. I felt like I should be careful and watch what we said or did (RED FLAG). Later that night when I was texting Chad, he asked if Cookie and her guy ever asked me to join them. I said of course not! Cookie and I were not like that. There were never any thoughts of us sharing anyone, we did not play that game. He then said he wished I would have kept on driving down to see him. If I did that, it would have been four to five more hours of driving, and my body was not having it. I only had one more day until I started working and I needed to be physically ready. There was no time to drive to Key West.

The next morning Chad woke me up with an early text. He said he had a bad dream about us, that we fell asleep together and when he woke up, I was gone. He said it scared him and had to text me right away (RED FLAG). I reassured him that I wasn't going anywhere. These exchanges were slightly unnerving, even though I thought it was cute that he was jealous or whatever it was. We would be better in person than over the phone anyway.

Before I left to drive back to Gainesville, Cookie told me that Chad seemed very intense and I needed to be careful, plus boat life was not easy and that she would never do it. I wanted her to see the Chad that I saw and trusted. I told her the boat life was not going to be forever. It was just a temporary thing until we could upgrade to a bigger houseboat and then to a house and then to rent the boats out. I did add that I would be careful, and Chad and I are so much alike and have the same goals and dreams, that we were going to have a fun and adventurous life together. I only wanted her support. I wasn't sure why I felt like I had to "sell" to one of my best friends on the guy I wanted a life with. (RED FLAG)

The next day I was texting Chad, telling him how we both have this energy about us to do whatever we want, that we both loved people and enjoyed entertaining. It was all so exhilarating to have a partner that was as crazy as yourself. As we were texting, I was thinking back to the first time we met. I told him that I felt the chemistry between us when we first met at his hotel, and I wanted to come back and see him that first night Cookie and I were in town. I was glad Cookie had a coffee date that next morning because that made me find his number to call him.

"And now look at us, planning our future," I said while smiling.

He replied, "Don't stop smiling cause I'm glad you called me the next day. I was hoping you girls would've come back that night. No big deal. We have forever now."

I would get butterflies in my stomach when he said sweet things like that. I have never felt so alive and hopeful and thrilled about what may lie ahead in my future.

Chad told me not to worry if he didn't answer right away because he was with his friend that he sold his BMW to, that he was signing over the title to him. So that means he would be without a car I thought.

Later Chad texted, "I had to go get the real dishes and appliances for the boat. I'm throwing the whole kitchen out and putting my stuff in there for us. Plus, I'm getting the bikes done up and things ready for us. This is a process hun. I'm bringing a whole life up there. Just have to get everything in order. Takes me a minute to shut me down in this area but I'm on it every day first thing in the morning. So, I can get up there to you asap."

I replied, "You are amazing, and I can't wait."

He added, "$1667.57 is what I just spent in fuel. LMFAO. She was thirsty. Well, this should easily get me there if no wind or I don't feel like tacking."
I told him I wish I could kiss him right then.

He said, "Soon hun, and I'm also quitting the liquid waste job to do this. Just so you know, I'm all in."

"I'm all in, too."

"Then hurry up and let's find a marina so we can be all in together. I'm looking now actually."

I told him on my days off I would look as well. At that moment though, it was time to get ready for my first day at work.

It was January 10th, and my first day of my first travel job. It was a twelve minute walk from the parking garage to the hospital. Quite a bit different from a two minute walk at my old job. I was feeling the vibe of the college atmosphere since Shand's was on the campus of the University of Florida. Hospital workers and students were hustling everywhere: walking or biking to and from the hospital. The air was warm and perfect with the sunrise peaking over the palm trees. I fell into step with the crowd as I was making my way into one of the hospital towers.

After finding where I had to go and almost getting lost, I felt like I was the oldest one there. Not only was I feeling old and out of place, but I was also having to learn a different computer charting system than what I was used to, and they had different equipment. Was this the same Shand's I used to work at? I didn't remember it being that big. At that point I was wondering what the hell did I get myself into! And will I ever find my way around this hospital!

When I worked at Shand's twenty years ago, there was only one tower. Now there were three, along with a tunnel under the street to cross between the towers. Everyone was super nice and there were a lot of travelers like me, but I was the new one: fresh into town, bottom of the list, the amateur, the novice, the "newbie," the first timer. First days at any job are always gut wrenching with everyone checking you out. I could feel the pressure to have to prove myself all over again. And then with Covid, we had to wear masks, so nobody could see my smile, they only saw the worry and fear in my eyes. There was so much to learn. I was hoping I had made the right choice.

That night after finding my way out of the hospital and back to my apartment, an apartment that

I shared with a stranger, I went into my bedroom, fell on my bed, broke down, and cried. I was so overwhelmed from the day's work and was wondering if I had made the right decision. I even wondered if that was what my daughter went through every time she moved into a new place while in college. There were so many new things to learn, new people, new place, new everything, it can be overwhelming for anyone.

I FaceTimed Chad shortly after that and he was patiently listening to me complain. Seeing him looking so concerned made me feel a little better. We didn't get to talk too much since I had to get some sleep for my next workday.

The next morning, he called me saying he couldn't sleep due to worrying about me and kept thinking of how he could make it better. One way would be to sail up sooner so we could be together every day. He said he couldn't wait to cook for me and even bring me to work. He repeated how he just wanted to breathe me in.

Later he texted, "Just so you know, that for our one year anniversary, we are sailing to the Bahamas. We would owe that to ourselves."

All that made me smile. Someone caring that much about me to want to be with me every day, to cheer me up and to breathe me in was the best feeling.

That afternoon he texted, "I think if you really want out of that field for good, then we should
68

eventually focus on the Airbnb as a life change. In time we can expand and offer services as well like jet ski tour, fishing charter. We already have the sailboat as a sailboat charter and sunset cruises. I'm just brainstorming because it hit a nerve seeing you all stressed out. I know you want to do Airbnb and drive a bus. Just a thought hun."

How sweet, he was trying to help me out by brainstorming ideas for our future. I still had twenty-five weeks to go and new things to learn, so at that point I was not really thinking that far ahead. It was one day at a time for me at that moment, but it was still sweet, and I really appreciated it.

As the days went by, work was getting a little easier with the help of some amazing therapists, nurses, and doctors. I was in the Medical Intensive Care Unit, and we were still in the midst of Covid working nonstop. UF Shands was a lot busier than I was used to, so my days flew by. I was learning so much, even though it was a little saturating at times, it was also challenging and rewarding. A couple weeks in I met another therapist around my age (finally!) who was also new to the traveling world. While talking, we found out we knew some of the same people and she had worked in the town near me and had a house in Nashville. We planned on a dinner date to get to know each other better. It was refreshing to finally start making friends. The world can be a lonely place without someone to talk to. I felt a slight weight lifted from my shoulders.

God puts people in our lives for different reasons and he was putting me and my new friend Julia together because we needed each other in that new place. We both believed that to be true.

It was January 16th, and time for wedding dress shopping in Alabama with my youngest daughter who was getting married in July. It was six hours to Birmingham, so off I went. I couldn't wait to see my daughters and go through the wedding dress shopping process one last time. I was telling Chad all about it on my way there. He said we could chauffeur them on the sailboat to the Bahamas for a wedding gift. I thought how marvelous that sounded, but I knew they already had plans. It felt good to have a partner that had an interest in my daughters, even if they are grown. I had also been telling my girls about Chad and our plans about living on a boat. I wanted them to like him and to be happy for me, and I was hoping they would all get to meet him soon. I wasn't entirely sure how or when that would happen, especially with the wedding planning going on and Chad trying to get the boat working for a big trip.

After a great time back in Alabama, it was time to come back to my new temporary home. On my way back I started thinking about what I could do to further prepare myself for a life on a boat. Doing research seemed like the best option, but I wanted to be able to keep what I find and to go back to it later. That gave me an idea. When I got back to Florida, I went to the bookstore and bought a few books on sailing, a couple sailing magazines, and a Florida day trip book. I was so excited and was hoping Chad would be impressed when I sent him a picture of my finds. Shoot, even *I* was impressed with my finds. I couldn't wait to hear what he had to say.

He texted back saying, "I'm sooooo exhausted. I seriously haven't felt like this in twenty years doing ops, I'm heading back to the boat and locking up. No visitors and I'm not leaving for two days."

I knew he had been extremely busy with the sailboat, getting it ready to sail and making it look nice, but I thought he'd at least acknowledge my photo of the books and magazines I purchased (RED FLAG). Slightly disappointed, I didn't say anything back about them and just told him to get some rest.

Soon after that I thought it would be a good idea to send him my location. When he asked if I was tracking him, I laughed a little. I wanted him to track me since I was doing a lot of driving back and forth to Alabama for wedding planning and birthday parties. He said I could track him too, that he had no problem with that. I thought that was a good idea, especially when he started to sail up to me. That seemed fun, being able to watch his icon move up north to me.

We started talking about bigger boats that we could live on and just use the sailboat for chartering and cruises. He sent me multiple ads of styles, sizes, etc. and he told me where to look. He was getting all excited that I was excited.

Every once in a while, I'd get nervous thinking about our future and living on a sailboat. Some people mentioned how crazy we were and how crazy I was since I've only known him for a short amount of time.

I'd express my concerns to Chad but let him know that I was not listening to them, that they were not us. The people talking didn't know how passionate we were and how we felt about this new life we wanted. I mentioned how I'm sure he was hearing the same things from his friends. He reassured me we were fine, that I was perfect for him, and not to worry, that he wasn't listening to his friends either.

It was January 28th, and I made another trip home for my grandson's third birthday party. I was really trying to keep up with family functions even though it was an eight hour drive each way. I didn't want to miss anything, and the drive was fun for me. The trips were also a good time to check in on my house. Sleeping in my own bed again always felt nice, too. Even though it was nice to see everyone, and the party turned out great, it was only a quick trip and I had to get back to work. That was the sad part I had to get used to: most trips back to visit were usually very short.

While on my drive back to Florida, Chad mentioned that he was helping his friends at Sloppy Joe's doing security and told me to go on the web cam and look for him. I told him as soon as I arrived back at my place that I would look. I watched him walk around doing what security guys do, but it was getting late, so I went to bed. He started working there almost every evening. We started missing each other for our usual morning conversations since we seemed to be on opposite schedules. He would text often about his nights.

One night he texted me, "Just had to use my ranger status against a navy seal. Drunk. LMFAO. He listened. I just wowed the crowd. LMFAO." (RED FLAG). I wasn't entirely sure what he meant by that, but I never asked about it.

He seemed to be working more and more at Sloppy Joe's and getting more and more tired. I started wondering when he would have time to get the boat ready to sail, since he made it sound like there was still a lot to do. I was feeling bad for him. He said they were hiring a couple new guys at Sloppy Joe's soon so he would have more time to work on the boat and then the sooner we could be together.

Looking at my calendar, I had a few days off in early February and decided to plan a trip to see Chad. He was overjoyed that I wanted to come down there. I told him how crazy it was to feel so passionate about someone, and how I've never felt like that before. I was telling him how I had never had anyone compliment me in front of others the way he has, and he had no idea how special that made me feel—so wanted. I thanked him for making my heart full and happy. He said it was because I WAS special and soon, he would show me just how much every day.

He was still working a few hours here and there helping out at Sloppy Joe's when he texted late one night saying, "I was busy last night. Bar fight. Took a shot to the back from some drunk. I'm ok. He isn't feeling too well. The other two guys involved in fight left with no issues. The guy that hit me in the back is on his way to the hospital, I'm ok. That's all that matters. Sleep well sweetheart."

Then about an hour later he texted again, "Damn. Two fights tonight. Just got a thank you from the police. Lol." (RED FLAG).

When I woke up and read my messages I was concerned and thankful he didn't get hurt. I asked if he was okay and how his back was feeling. He said a little sore but not bad. He added that he was going to tell the owner at Sloppy Joe's that he was giving him until Friday to find someone to work, that he was done helping. Good, I thought. With all the tourists that go there I was sure there were a fair number of fights that happened, and I didn't want him to get hurt.

We would face time every few days and talk about our plans and dreams some more. It was definitely something to look forward to and seeming more real each time we talked. I told him I was going to bring some of my stuff down to put on the boat. I had been going through my stuff and downsizing every time I went home, looking through my cabinets, closets, and drawers. I found things we might could use on our boat and things I didn't need anymore. He told me to bring whatever I wanted, but within reason. I could put all my stuff in one of the bedrooms and eventually we could gut it and make it one huge closet. That sounded like a perfect plan to me. We also talked about how this sailboat was only temporary, and we would have to look into a storage unit. I thought, yeah, mostly for all my stuff. Even with downsizing as many times as I had done, I still had a lot of things.

I was getting nervous not hearing from Chad for almost two days when he finally texted back saying he dropped his new phone on the curb and cracked the screen. He said he felt like skipping it off into the ocean, and that he couldn't wait for us to be together so I could be the keeper of his phone once and for all (RED FLAG). He apologized for being so clumsy. I told him I have never known anyone who had so many issues with their phone. Half the time he had no charge, which I could understand because when I was trying to charge my phone on his sailboat, it took forever, and it almost never took a full charge. The other half of the time he lost it, broke it, or had it stolen. It seemed like a lot of bad luck to me.

We were both getting excited to see each other in a few days. Chad told me to bring whatever I wanted onto the boat and that if I had any extra DVDs to bring them, too. He added that there were a few people that wanted to meet me, and we might go to dinner with one of the couples the night I arrived. He said it had been a while since he had been with anyone, so all his friends were thrilled and happy for him that he found someone that seemed like a good fit for him. I was counting down the days before I got to see the man of my dreams again.

Chapter 6

(Key West)

It was February 7th, and time for my first road trip to Key West in my truck. I loaded up some blankets, pillows, towels, DVD's, a few small items that would be perfect for on a boat, and a cooler with my lunch and snacks in it. Red (my truck) and I took off. It was an eight hour drive. I have always loved road trips. And since I wasn't living at my house in Alabama, my truck was the main thing that I felt connected to and the most comfortable in. I had recently traded my car in for Red, since I knew I'd be traveling a lot, and I thought a truck would be more practical with the room in the bed. She was only a year old with only 3,000 miles on her and it happened to be my favorite color. We have become best friends. With this travel assignment, I was planning on having her paid off in a couple months. I had her windows tinted and a back cover put on the bed. My brother made me a couple hitch covers, a Seahawks one and one that says, Bad Girlz Toy.

I particularly love road trips with palm trees lining the highway. You definitely get that view driving through the state of Florida. There was something enjoyable and calming seeing the palm trees on the road, and it made me happy. The drive from Key Largo to Key West was the best in my opinion, with its one hundred thirteen miles of scenic Highway. It's a slow drive traveling through forty-four islands and over forty-two bridges, taking about two to three hours. It's one of the most beautiful places in Florida and definitely worth that time. I enjoyed having the ocean on both sides while driving down the middle. It's also one of the most tropical places I've ever been. If anyone wanted to get away and go somewhere tropical, then the Florida Keys would be it. Many years ago, when I lived in Florida, my ex-husband and I would take a weekend and drive down to Key West and stay in the military trailers on White Street. They were in the middle of Key West which made it a perfect getaway. I enjoyed Key West then but was appreciating it so much more since I have aged. And for the first time driving down by myself, it was a new experience, one that I was truly savoring. I was soaking up the sites and the sun. It seems we appreciate life's beauty so much more when we get older.

I arrived in Key West early that afternoon. I met Chad and after our kisses and hugs, he introduced me to Missy and Michael, the couple that was going to take us to his boat since his dinghy was still out of commission. They were super nice and to find out, Missy lived on her own boat and Michael lived on his own boat. Chad said we were going to take them to dinner for helping us. We had a nice time, and Missy and I got along great. She was an artist in town who painted murals and I did woodwork, so we related to one another. Her dreadlocks and tan suited her well, I thought. Later I found some of her work in a local brewery and I was amazed at her talent, and I was surprised she didn't have a shop there selling her artwork. Dinner was great and after Chad paid for all of us, he then gave them some money for helping us to his boat. Missy helped me carry some of the stuff I brought to put on the sailboat.

She said, "This is what we do quite often living on a boat, we load and unload, load and unload."

I could see that to be true. After they left, Chad and I relaxed on the boat enjoying each other. I had brought Chad a couple gifts; one from Christmas and one for Valentine's Day. He said nobody ever gave him anything and the gifts I brought made him feel so special. He gave me a pooka shell necklace that he found on the boat (RED FLAG). I didn't think too much about it knowing he was fixing up the boat and doing all this for me. I also knew he didn't have time to go out shopping for gifts, so I accepted the gaudy thing knowing I was not going to be wearing it other than right then.

When we started catching up with each other and talking, Chad told me that he was in the process of changing his last name from his mother's German side to his stepdad's Italian side, since his stepdad was in the middle of writing his will and making it official. However, he would not have Chad in the will if he did not change his name back to the Italian name his stepdad had. His stepdad traveled a lot and bought land/houses everywhere he went, and Chad explained: "Once my name is changed, one day we will be inheriting all the land when my stepdad passes away. He's a millionaire and has land in Costa Rica, Puerto Rico, Bahamas, and a few more places in the Caribbean." Since Chad basically grew up in these places, he would be the only one of his siblings to inherit the land, while the others would just be getting money. All because Chad was the only one who appreciated going to those places. So now Chad had to change his driver's license, passport, all his bank accounts, and all the other cards he had. He said it was a process and was going to take a while. Chad planned on changing his name back to his mother's side, right after he showed his stepdad all the documents with his new name and signed the papers for the will. He hated his stepdad and how he was making him change his name (RED FLAG).

The next day Chad took me to one of the other islands for dinner and Putt-Putt. We had so much fun together. It was like we had known each other for years and fell right back in rhythm as if we hadn't been apart. He seemed to be good at everything. Who knew he could golf? So of course, I did not win. While I was driving on the way back to Key West, I showed Chad my GoPro. He got excited about it and was trying to figure out how it worked, so he tried videoing. I thought it was cute that he was that interested. We made it back in town and after parking, we ran into some of Chad's acquaintances from the hotel on our walk to the marina. One gentleman asked if I was his wife and Chad looked at me saying, "hopefully soon." (RED FLAG). It was a lot to take in, but I was enjoying all the attention he gave me and how I seemed to be the number one in his life. He said nobody else mattered to him, and that he had been faithful since the day we met, and even though he had told me that before, I was loving all of it the same.

After getting back on the boat, we enjoyed each other's presence while talking about everything and anything under the sun. Chad told me besides doing security at Sloppy Joe's, he also worked for a guy who hired him on the spot to work security for some of the famous people that own yachts or islands there in Key West including Kenny Chesney and JZ and Beyonce (RED FLAG). I looked both of them up and Kenny Chesney does go down there a lot and JZ and Beyonce do own a yacht that stays in Key West often. He had a great security clearance from being a ranger for twenty years, so it wouldn't surprise me that he would do security for the famous.

He also opened up and became emotional telling me about some of the people he had to dispatch while in the military. He told me he tried to not think about those times, but they were always there. He would get very offended by those who impersonated the military, and he could tell when they were faking it. I listened to his stories and was thinking, what a well-rounded, diverse, interesting man Chad was.

He told me that he just wanted us to be together every day and that he couldn't wait to put a ring on it! I had never had anyone talk about wanting to be with me that much and it felt amazing. I was wanted. He said he would do anything for me and that he was willing to change for me. Whatever I wanted, that I was his girl. I liked how he said that. I was "His girl."

We laid down the bench in the living room that made into a couch that night, cuddled and watched a movie. It felt so warm and cozy and comfortable and right. The way he touched me so gently and then the kisses on the forehead, for some reason, those kisses made me melt. I felt protected and special. With the constant breeze of the ocean and the occasional seagull, it was perfect. All natural. I was thinking of how easy I could get used to that.

He decided to tell me that he was going to sail up to be with me and that he was starting to get everything ready. He was ready to be with me every day all day. He already quit two jobs for me and leaving Key West for me (RED FLAG). I was still in awe that this man was so into me that he was giving up his life there in Key West for me. I felt like a princess. Somebody wanted me that much, to give up what they had to start a life elsewhere. I wasn't sure how to take it, but I was going to go for it. Love doesn't happen too often in this lifetime, so embrace it when you can, is what my heart was saying.

We also brainstormed about our life when my contract was over. Chad had mentioned the idea of us sailing to the Gulf of Mexico to be closer to my family. I realized that he was actually thinking of me and my family. I didn't have to bring it up this time, like in my previous relationships. That meant the world to me. Because when the day is over, I have kids who are a huge part of me. I was a package deal.

The next day I met one of Chad's friends named Tom. He came out to the boat to help Chad with getting the dinghy working. Tom sailed down from Michigan after retiring. He was in his 60's and seemed like a really nice, genuine guy. Chad said he got Tom a job at Sloppy Joe's, and they were like brothers, they helped each other out when needed. I thought that was awe-inspiring, to have a friend like that.

It was now time for me to drive back to Gainesville and Chad asked if I could drop him off at the police station since he had to appear at court for a traffic violation (RED FLAG). I had no problem with that. He put his best clothes on and after getting a ride to shore, off we went. Our goodbyes seemed to be getting harder and harder. But knowing we would be together soon helped. It was time to get back to work and to make plans on looking for a marina near me. One day Chad would be close enough where I could call the boat my home and crawl into bed with him after a twelve hour day at work. I loved the thought of that: someone to go home to at the end of the day. Someone who loved me as much as I loved them. Someone to spend forever with.

As I was driving back to work, Chad was texting me telling me to come back, that it's not too late to turn around.

I said, "Are you sure you want this old gal to be your copilot?"

"After some fine tuning, yes, most definitely." We both laughed. I couldn't wait to get out there and look for a marina for us. Maybe I would get my captain's license. I was already trying to learn all the boating lingo. If a boat is where I'm going to be, then I

83

needed to learn everything I could. That excited me. The first thing I needed to do was to look for a marina, so I decided on my next day off of work I would do just that.

Chapter 7

(Marinas)

After a few days of work, I had some days off and decided to drive to Crystal River, Florida on the Gulf side, which was the closest waterway to Gainesville. It would also be a better area to sail up to and be out of the way from most hurricanes. They had an impressive marina online and I wanted to visit it in person. When I arrived, I envisioned myself watching the manatees swim around the boat, then riding my bike into town. It was perfect. Chad gave me all the dimensions of the boat to tell the dock master to see if there was a spot for the sailboat. After talking to the dock master, he let me know that they did not have a slip deep enough for the sailboat, and the ones out in the water on a mooring ball were already taken. That was discouraging, especially since I really liked it there. I realized then that this was not going to be an easy task. It was even more difficult without Chad there with me to agree or disagree on a marina. For me being a soon-to-be first time boat person, I really wanted to be tied up on a dock so I could get off when I wanted and to use their facilities. I also needed to be able to walk off and go straight to work rather than depending on a dinghy to get me to shore first. And what if it rained? I would have to wear a waterproof jumpsuit to keep from getting my scrubs soaked. The thought of that was not pretty. So, with this one scratched off the list, I still had many more to go.

That following weekend I was free from work, so I had a friend from Palatka, Florida ride with me to

Jacksonville, Florida to look at marinas there. One was creepy looking on a dirt road with no way in hell I'd live there, one was too fancy and expensive, and another one was all booked up with no room. it was getting frustrating and harder than I thought. I had a great time visiting with my friend, but it was back to the drawing board. The next place to look would be St. Augustine, Florida. That would be further away than our original plan, but I could definitely see myself living there. It was such a fun little town, and the oldest one in the United States. They even had a beach you could drive on. That was also the place outside of Palatka, where I lived for about five years with my ex-husband and three girls. St. Augustine was definitely okay in my books.

It was the middle of February now and my new friend Julia from work happily joined me to go look at marinas in St. Augustine. I remembered to grab my GoPro to start documenting my side of mine and Chad's love story. Off we went! The first marina was too expensive, and the parking was first-come, first-served, so you might have to park some blocks away. The next one was full, with a waiting list. After talking to the owner of that marina, she said we would be lucky to find any marina with even one available spot, at that time or even in the near future. Ever since Covid, everyone wanted to live on a boat, so every marina was full. With Chad saying that he could sail up as soon as the next month, I needed one soon. It was getting very unrealistic at that point. There was one marina left in St. Augustine to look at within a reasonable price. We pulled in and found the dock master and started asking questions. He had one slip available that would fit the size of Chad's sailboat, but said it was first-come first-served with them going fast. Julia and I loved the area, and I could picture myself living at that marina. The dock master showed us the slip we would have, right next to another sailboat. I could ride my bike or jog into town or take the scooter to the beach and even take the dinghy out to the local restaurants that were on the water. It looked like so much fun. I have always enjoyed St. Augustine, with its cobblestone roads, the old houses with their Spanish architecture, charming restaurants as well as the tranquil beaches, and to top it off, my favorite winery. Both Julia and I felt like that was it, the one. I had to act fast, so I went ahead and paid the deposit. I knew Chad would be excited and pay me back. I signed some papers and secured our spot (RED FLAG). I knew Chad had been spending a lot of money on getting everything ready, so I hated to ask for the money from him at that moment. I was ecstatic and nervous at the same time knowing how real everything was getting. I was envisioning myself finding my own little coffee shop, jogging, and biking around like a local. I even thought of bringing my potted palm tree to place underneath the gazebo for everyone to enjoy.

Julia and I decided to celebrate by eating out at a nice seafood restaurant on the water nearby. It would be so easy to park the dinghy there and have a nice meal once Chad and I were living at the marina. They also had food trucks parked at the marina certain days of the week. We definitely wouldn't starve. Julia and I left there and went to the San Sebastián winery to continue our celebration. I was talking to one of the bartenders there while sampling the wines and she said they were building a dock at the winery and that I'd be able to bring the dinghy over. How enjoyable that would be! All of it was sounding like a dream. I was texting Chad, telling him everything and he was excited also, but more focused on getting the boat ready to sail.

A couple of days went by, and I had not heard from Chad. The last he texted was that he was back working at Sloppy Joe's and super busy. He had been in touch with the dock master at the marina I picked out and Chad said for me to help fill out the paperwork since he didn't have a printer. He wanted to use my address since he was leaving his and that I was his contact person (RED FLAG). That all made sense to me at the time.

I was telling my friends at work that I was planning on living on a boat soon in St. Augustine, and they could see how excited I was and how I was glowing. They were all happy for me and very supportive. I invited them to visit once Chad and I were settled in.

It was the second half of February, and the marina rent was already due for the month of March. Since the spot was in my name and my card was on file from the deposit, the marina took $925.00 out of my account. I let Chad know about it and I trusted that he would pay me back as soon as his bank cleared him from his name change (RED FLAG).

My time in the apartment was soon ending,

and since I waited too late to rebook it for more time during my work contract, it was already booked up. Chad said it was only a little while longer before sailing up to me, giving me a place to live, so with that life within my reach, I was confident he would sail up in time for me to move onto the boat and not have to pay one more month's rent at a random place.

As the days went by with no word on Chad sailing, and with the move out day coming up, I was getting nervous about where I would live. Chad was my only plan, so if he didn't come up in time, what was I going to do? When I told Julia about my predicament, she happily invited me to stay with her for the time being. Relief washed over me, and of course I would take her up on that offer! Everything was working out in my favor, and I felt good about my life again.

When Chad finally said he was ready to sail, he had his friend Tom all set to sail up with him, and they were both excited to see me. Tom said he would cook us a nice meal when he and Chad finally arrived in St. Augustine. They were even looking forward to having me show them around the new town. The only thing slowing everything down was the weather. It seemed that once things were finally ready to go, the weather was blocking Chad and Tom from leaving, so then we all had to wait a few more days for the skies to clear.

After settling in at Julia's apartment, we watched the movie The Tinder Swindler together, about how one guy managed to convince women to send him money over the dating app. I was blown away at how those women just gave him money, without really getting to know him. They took out loans and handed over thousands of dollars, and they were never able to retrieve their money back since they willingly handed it over to the guy. I couldn't believe how desperate and foolish these girls were. This guy is still out there because there's not anything they can do about it. All I could think was how insane the whole story was. People are crazy and they could do that here in the United States, not just Europe. I was dumbfounded about the whole circumstance. Julia and I talked a little bit about it over the next day or two, it stayed on our minds.

A few more days went by not hearing from Chad. I texted him to tell him that I watched the Tinder Swindler on Netflix, and I started getting a little paranoid, because that could happen anywhere. Even though I did not meet Chad on Tinder, there's no telling who would pull a stunt like that. I've heard of lots of unreal or bad things happening around me, but no one I personally knew went through anything like that. With that being said, when I didn't hear from Chad, my mind would wander. He finally called me saying he took the boat out and let a friend steer it, and it got all tangled up in some chain underneath and tore the boat up. So now he was going to have to take it in to a dry dock to put it on stilts and start working on it again. He was so upset and mad at his friend. I just listened and let him vent. Maybe it was a good thing, to get it double checked before sailing. In that case I was a little happy to have it up on stilts and I hoped the damage wasn't too bad.

In the meantime, I had a trip planned to Sea World with a coworker named Selena. We had a great time together and I told Chad about us getting to ride the roller coasters as much as we wanted since the lines were so short. He said soon we would be able to go to those parks together, and his main life goal was to see Optimus Prime at Universal Studios, and after that he could die in peace. That made me think, since I was planning on meeting one of my daughters and her family in Orlando on their trip to Disney in May, maybe Chad should go with me. That way on one of the days we aren't with them in Disney, we could go and spend a day at Universal Studios where he could finally see Optimus Prime. It excited me to make one of his dreams come true. We would have so much fun! We would finally get to have some time together and get to have a little adventure on our own that didn't involve the boat and its current problems. I already couldn't wait.

The next day Chad was telling me about how beautiful the sailboat was up on stilts and that he was recording it all for his side of our love story. He said there were a few moments in there that he was cursing me because he was doing all this for the love of his life…Me. He seemed in good spirits even though he said that had been costing him some money and he was already twenty grand into it (RED FLAG).

That night when working at Sloppy Joe's Chad managed to get in the middle of a bar fight. He said he took himself to the hospital because he thought he had a couple broken ribs (RED FLAG—another fight).

I told him to be careful now that he had a girlfriend. He said, "girlfriend? Future wife." That made me blush.

The following day, the dock master where I reserved the boat slip was asking for all the information on the sailboat. I was needing Chad to send me a copy of the registration and a copy of his driver's license. He said all of that was on the boat and that he would send it to me as soon as he could. He added that he was waiting for the magistrate to file the paperwork over to him since it was a death, his best friend. He said I would meet Sam, the son of that friend soon. He sent over the boat information minus his driver's license (RED FLAG), and he said he would now start the process of leaving to come up to St. Augustine. I thought, finally!

A little later Chad mentioned that the guy he sold his Beamer to wanted to trade it for the new dinghy Chad just bought. He said his friend had been begging to trade lately, so if he did, then I would have to drive back down in my truck to Key West, so I could attach the BMW, and drive back up to the marina so we both would have our own vehicles. I didn't know that Chad had bought a new dinghy, or what happened to the old one he had. Either way, you need one so you can get from your houseboat on the water to the docks on land. The dinghy acts like a car, but on the water. I wanted to ask him more details, but I thought otherwise since it wasn't my money, and I didn't think it was my place to say anything, either.

He said, "We will have a truck, an SUV, a bike

(scooter), a dinghy, and a boat. A good start, all bought and paid for." I thought so too, so I didn't ask my questions.

Chad had a new friend he was paying to sail up with him since Tom said he couldn't take off work anymore. The days seemed to fly by, and it was getting close to the end of February.

The next time we talked, Chad told me he was thirty grand into his sailboat (RED FLAG), and it seemed everything was going wrong: now he was needing new batteries, and the wiring was all messed up. He said that he hated to keep complaining about the money, but he was not used to dipping into accounts that he had not used before, and it was starting to stress him out. My thoughts were that I was out money, too, since I paid for the marina fee, and that I never once asked for him to sail up to me; that was all on him. Plus, if he had rental money coming in and never touched his pension, then he should be fine. I never said any of that aloud, I just listened and kept my thoughts to myself. Looking back now, I know I should have said something (RED FLAG).

It seemed like one issue turned into another. My patience was starting to wear. I knew he was getting frustrated also, so I sent him a picture of me dressed up going out to dinner with Julia to cheer him up. He always knew what to say and it never failed to make me smile right back. Most of the time he would say I was still beautiful, that there was never a bad light, or that my smile brightened up the picture. I asked if he had a book telling him what to say, and he replied, "No book hun, it's just what comes out because of the way you make me feel."

That made me smile and feel warm inside. I'd tell him what restaurants Julia and I were trying out and he mentioned for me to take notes because he wanted to go to all those restaurants too. I said of course I would, and I couldn't wait until the day we were together trying out new places as a couple, either by car, bike, or boat. That would be so amazing to do with the one you're crazy about.

While at dinner with Julia, Chad texted saying, "We are now proud owners of a BMW hun. My old BMW that is, she's a good SUV. We can trade her in on a convertible for you when you get your truck all paid for."

He knew I had been working hard at putting extra money on my truck to have it paid off in a few months. How sweet of him to think of me and wanting to get me a convertible. That would be later on down the road of course, right now he needed to get the boat ready to sail.

It was the night before Chad's birthday, and I told him I had a birthday present for him. He said the only thing he wanted was me, and soon, real soon. He could tell I was getting very anxious and tired of waiting for him to sail up.

He said, "Sweetheart, do not get discouraged, we will be together soon. I want nothing more than you and me together. Forever."

"Thank you," I said. "I want that too and I wish I had your patience."

All the paperwork was in and signed and so we were officially renting a slip at a marina in St. Augustine. Chad said he would start plotting out the course for his sail up. He said how excited he was and told me what a great job I did securing the slip, that I was awesome. Then he mentioned for me to not leave him for one of my co-workers (RED FLAG). I was a little confused as to why he would say that, but I laughed a little bit and told him I wouldn't have paid money to secure a slip if I was going to leave him.

A few days later Chad asked if I was having second thoughts about us.

I said, "No, are you?"

"No, I'm excited about the whole thing, I just wanted to make sure we were still on the same page," he said. I didn't think much of it after that.

It was the last day of February, and I took a trip home for a few days to see my girls. I also took my books about sailboats and was learning how to tie knots. When practicing, I would show one of my daughters how to do one and she tried. We laughed since it took a long time for either one of us to get it right, not just one time, but multiple times. I tried to impress Chad with some of the terms and names I was learning.

"Knot that I'll remember all of these," I texted.

"You're knot funny!" he responded.

We went back and forth joking about knots, making lots of puns and whatnots. He said bowline is easy, that he'd teach me, and that he liked to use the half hitch and clove hitch. I made a mental note to make sure I learned those.

My neighbors Jacob and Dawn stopped by a little later that evening and I called Chad on FaceTime to meet them. It was important to me for Chad and them to get along because when I first moved into that house, those neighbors came to greet me. They were close to the age of my parents, and soon we became like family. Jacob and Dawn would invite me over with most of their family functions and treated me like one of their own. I call them my stepparents. After I told them about Chad, they were a little worried about me falling for him so fast, and I respected their concerns and opinions. I was a little nervous about them meeting Chad because I didn't know what anyone was going to say. Jacob and Dawn asked Chad what his intentions were with me, and I immediately felt like a high schooler all over again. I listened to hear what Chad would say, and he answered that he just wanted to be with me and breathe me in. I think they were expecting him to say that he was going to take care of me and marry me. The conversations seemed to go well, and I felt as if Jacob and Dawn approved, even though we didn't talk much about it afterwards. They knew I was head-over-heels for this guy, so they probably kept their thoughts to themselves.

It was time to get back to work and wait on Chad to sail up. We were into March now and he was still working a lot at Sloppy Joe's and fixing multiple things on the boat. He said he bought a new mooring ball for the boat that he'd be bringing up with him and he was going to leave his old one with Jerry. When we decide to sail back down to Key West, we could just get it back from Jerry.

It seemed like the days were flying by and Chad was still waiting on parts or working. He was getting more exhausted with each passing day. I tried not to bother him too much, so I focused on all the activities coming up with my youngest daughter's wedding. I was starting to wonder how I was going to get Chad up North to meet my three daughters. My daughters are very important to me, and so was my life in Alabama. I wanted Chad to know all about that life in Alabama and to get to know my kids and family there. I also wanted my kids to see what I saw in Chad. To see how I would want a future with this amazing man who adored me and wanted to be with me every day and to build a business and life together. I wanted them to be included and happy for me, but I wanted their support most of all.

Chad seemed to be getting close to being ready to sail and wanted me to write down the weather report for Key West, Miami, and St. Augustine for the next week in nautical terms. I wrote down the winds, knots, and sea swells. Some swells were 4-6ft at times. Chad says those turn into 8-9ft swells usually, but that he was planning on leaving soon even with the rough seas. I started getting more excited with how real it seemed for him and the boat to be finally ready to come up!

We FaceTimed quite often, and Chad was getting anxious but excited about setting sail. He expressed how he was getting discouraged with how much this was costing him, that it was out of his comfort zone because he wasn't used to worrying about money (RED FLAG). He said he'd have to get two jobs when he made it to St. Augustine. With how hard he of a worker he was, I didn't doubt he'd have a job lined up within days of arriving in St. Augustine. People gravitated toward him regularly, and he loved being around people just as much as I did, so I believed he needed a job anyway for the days I would work. It would do him good, especially in a new town. We discussed using the sailboat as a charter business and buying a yacht to live on. He joked about me selling my house to buy a yacht (RED FLAG). That idea turned into a bigger idea, and soon enough he was telling me to focus on looking at yachts I liked. While I did that, he said he would focus on getting up to St. Augustine, getting our business started, and us being together every day.

On March 10th, I made another trip home to celebrate my twin daughters' birthday that weekend. I was definitely putting some miles on Red. Red and I had a routine when driving home. I had my spots picked out during my drive on where I would take a small stretch break, where I wanted to stop and eat, where the best coffee was and where to take the extra 30 minute scenic route if I wanted. It was nice to have options.

At the end of March Chad told me that he'd be waking up next to me in the next week. He was getting a cooler ready with food to last a week for him and his new co-pilot. It was almost time for him to set sail! We were both very anxious. The weather seemed to change every minute with it being fine one minute to heavy winds the next. I kept my fingers crossed that he would pull up the anchor any day and be on his way. My little sailor man, leaving Key West for me. For us to start a business and a life together. We would be the perfect hosts for chartering and Airbnb. We would fix the sailboat up, get our captains licenses and charter people out for sunset cruises to start off with. Meeting people from all over the world sounded so enjoyable to me. I loved hearing other people's stories. Plus, by then we would have our own story to tell. Everything seemed to be finally falling into place.

The marina sent me a bill for the month of April, since I initially paid for it on my card. After I paid it, I sent a screenshot of it to Chad to let him know so he would realize that I had paid for two months' rent now, something I hadn't planned on initially, and hoped he would pay me back soon. He never acknowledged it (RED FLAG).

Shortly after I sent the screenshot, he sent me a video of the sunrise from the bow saying, "Today's the day, the famous Key West saying, today's the day, that's what Mel Fisher used to say. So, today's the day we set sail, so let's see where she winds up."

That made me forget about the marina fees, instead I was excited knowing today's the day! Nothing would make me happier than getting to see the boat sail into the marina. I was beyond ready for this sail to begin. It gave me chills just thinking about it. I've fallen for this guy and at that moment I wanted him to know exactly how I felt, especially before he was out at sea where he would probably lose cell service. I texted him about how excited I was and that there was something I had been wanting to tell him. I wanted to wait and tell him in person, but I couldn't wait any longer. I wanted him to know that I loved him. I wanted him to know that I loved him before he lost service out in the ocean. I waited for his response with my heart beating out of my chest. About five hours passed by and no text from Chad (RED FLAG). A little worried that I may have said something wrong, I finally texted and asked if everything was okay. He said he was doing last minute things. He said he sent Tom inland for sandwiches and that him and Billy (his new co-pilot) would be leaving a little later that day. He said they'd be leaving headwind up to Miami, so he'd be using the motor and have to refuel there. After that they would catch winds the next day. He then sent me a video of his goodbye song to key west and a picture of his bicycle on board. We would have to come back for the scooter he said, it was too heavy and awkward to get it on board. He never did acknowledge my "I love you" text (RED FLAG).

I asked Chad if I could track his location so I would know where he was out in the ocean. He said no problem and let me add him right away. That would ease my mind some, to know where he was while sailing up to me.

A day went by with no text from Chad, and I was wondering if he was backing out on me. I asked him what was up and told him everything I'd been doing on my end to make all this happen. After securing the marina, I had been downsizing and the backseat of my truck was loaded down with stuff that would be finding a home on the boat. Waiting to hear from Chad to find out what was happening on his end was so worrisome. Eventually he said he was not backing out, that he was only frustrated. A little later he called me to tell me he needed a few new batteries, and he was waiting for them to come in from Miami. I was glad he was finally filling me in on the details. I tried my hardest not to ask too many questions since I knew he was frustrated. I was confused, because why would he have told me he was leaving, just to tell me he needed new batteries? It seemed he was communicating less and less, and I was getting worried about him. When Chad would finally answer my texts and missed calls, he'd tell me his phone was dead and needed charging, or he left it on the boat while he was on land. All this was making my stomach turn. It had been three days since the morning he said he was leaving. I decided to look on the web cam at Sloppy Joe's one evening and saw him working (RED FLAG). He wasn't telling me anything and now I was getting frustrated. I let him know I saw him working and I was glad to know he was okay since I had not heard from him lately. I also let him know how he hurt me by not talking, and I was beginning to wonder if he was doing that on purpose.

That was not a good start of a relationship. I added how I was trying to hold it together, but not knowing what his plans were was driving me crazy.

He said, "The windstorms kept us here and the batteries sealed the deal until I get them, they are ordered. Winds are horrendous down here."

None of that really made me feel better. It would have been nice to be hearing it in person and not waiting to hear it in a text, especially after practically begging or forcing him to talk to me.

I was willing to work on our relationship, so I kept trying to communicate. I let Chad know I thought about going down to see him, and if he was okay with it. I would then trade with Julia a couple days so I could visit. He said he was working all the nights I mentioned (RED FLAG). That was disappointing, and I certainly felt like he was shutting me out.

"It feels like you're leaving me in the dark and idk if you're doing it on purpose or not, but we are in this together. I can't have us if it's just me," I text him.

"I'm sorry, you're right. I'll try to get better about keeping you informed. I've just been super frustrated with everything, the batteries haven't come in yet, there's been some storms, it seems like everything is up against me. I just feel like I'm stuck and helpless. I'm sorry I haven't made it up to you yet, hun." He seemed super upset and I could tell, so I tried to encourage him as best as I could.

He added, "I've been trying so hard to make this work for us and make this dream a reality for you, but everything is just going wrong. There's always something going wrong and when that thing is fixed, it's another thing. Now, I've lost my wallet and can't get any money from the bank until things are clear from my name change, and I can't even do anything anyway because the banks are all closed from the storms."

We Facetimed after that and he was telling me he didn't want me to see him this defeated, that he felt like he was letting me down. Chad even mentioned how he stopped helping out the locals. Since they weren't getting any money from Chad, they weren't helping him at all. He had been trying to get a ride back to the boat, but nobody was willing to help. Since a recent bad storm, he had been stuck on the island for a few days. Hearing and seeing how upset he was on our video call was really hard for me. Right before he said goodbye, tears were filling his eyes. I felt so bad that I wanted to cry too.

After some time of feeling sad, I decided to act. I decided at that moment we needed to see each other, and I was going to go down there whether he liked it or not. My man needed me, and I was going to be there for him. It was time to pack for another road trip to Key West.

Chapter 8

(Maggots)

It was early morning April 4th, and I was all packed and ready to head to Key West to cheer up my man. Nobody needed to be down and out at that point; we both have worked hard to make everything happen. I ate breakfast, watered my plants, left a note for Julia, and then took off! After a couple hours of listening to my music and waiting for Chad to awaken, I called him and let him know I was on my way to see him. At first, he didn't believe me, even when we video called. It took a lot of convincing before he finally realized I was serious, and then he grew excited. He even said he would call in sick to work the next couple nights so we could spend some real time together. I was looking forward to that too.

When I let him know that I was getting close to town, we decided to meet in a shopping center parking lot. I couldn't wait to give him the biggest hug ever. It seemed like the longest drive getting to the parking lot. I finally found it and found him waiting for me, but my heart ached when I saw him. He looked rough: slightly skinnier than I remembered, with the slightest hint of dark shadows under his eyes, and his hair wasn't as neat as it usually was.

After hugging and some kissing with some small talk about my drive, I asked if he wanted to get some lunch and he said, "I'm fine, but you can get something."

"When was the last time you ate something?" I asked. It seemed unusual for him to turn down a meal.

"Oh, I don't know. I think yesterday at some point," Chad said.

I was a little concerned, but I tried not to let it show. I just said, okay and looked around for a place nearby. There was an Outback in the shopping center so I said we would eat there. I knew he had no wallet or money, but we both needed to eat. Him more than myself. While having steak and potatoes he said he couldn't believe that I was actually there and that nobody had done anything like that for him ever before. That made me feel good, but sad for him. I feel like that's what you do in a relationship, and I'm sure he'd do the same for me.

I asked where he had been sleeping. Looking a little ashamed, he said, "The mangroves." That's where the homeless sleep. I felt so sad for him. I knew we needed to get to a hotel next. He needed a shower and a bed.

It was time to find somewhere to stay once our bellies were full. He recommended a certain hotel on Duval Street that was nice. All hotels in Key West are expensive so I figured what the heck, sounds good to me. Parking of course was the hardest part, and after paying on my phone for parking, while checking in, we found out the hotel had free parking across the street. There was $20.00 wasted. I shrugged it off, as long as we were cozy for the night it was okay with me.

We took turns showering and Chad took the longest shower I have ever witnessed. It made me wonder when he showered last. He had a few clothes in his scooter, but everything else was on the boat. I sat on the bed and waited until he was dressed and felt much better before suggesting what to do that night.

We had to stay clear of Sloppy Joe's since he called in sick. We people watched while looking over the hotel balcony and then relaxed in the pool while enjoying the sunset. It was a beautiful night in Key West as usual, and we both slept like babies after a night of cuddling and touching. My heart was full and happy to be lying next to the man I loved. We woke to the roosters crowing and Chad had asked for a few dollars to go across the street to get some cigarettes. He still planned on quitting for me, but with all the stress lately, he wasn't able to give them up just yet.

I had some fruit in my cooler, and he said to bring it and he would take me to a nice little place on the Atlantic side that was perfect for a picnic. He took me into the Tropical Forest and Botanical Gardens. With all the tropical flowers, trees, and plants, it truly was a perfect paradise. We found a bench to eat our fruit on while looking out at the ocean. It was heavenly. It was like we were the only ones around. I wished every day could be that peaceful.

Later for lunch, Chad wanted me to try out this healthy bowl place called Grain and Berry Cafe. It was my first time having a healthy fruit bowl with granola, honey and berries. I loved the fact that Chad wanted to be healthy by riding his bike and eating right. He kept saying how amazing we were going to look after we got all settled together. We would be bike riding, going to a gym, walking every day, and eating healthy. That sounded ideal to me.

We took our time walking around and talking about our future. Chad was trying to get us a ride out to his boat, so he made a few phone calls during that time. I wanted some seafood, so we decided to go to a restaurant on the beach near the botanical gardens called Salute. While waiting for a table, Chad leaned against a pole and jumped, I thought maybe a lizard, or something bit him. I decided to touch the same pole, one that still had Christmas lights wrapped around it, and it shocked me which made me jump also.

He said, "I was about to tell you not to do that cause it'll shock you, but you did it anyways."

We both laughed so hard at ourselves. We seemed to have fun no matter where we went. The waiter told us to follow her to our table and she grabbed another couple at the same time. We giggled after whispering how we should sit down with them and squeeze in and act like nothing was wrong. Of course, we didn't, but the thought of what they would think made us giggle and laugh. It's like we had the same thoughts. We already walked the same, which we noticed on the way there. We just fit. Our thoughts, goals, dreams, sense of humor, our personalities, and our bodies.

As we received our crab legs, Chad received a phone call saying his friend was ready to take us to his boat. He told him we were on our way. Because of that, we had to scarf down our food and pay before we could head over to the docks, plus find a parking spot. By the time all that happened, his friend was not happy with us. Luckily, he took us to the boat anyway. I had to give him $20.00 for giving us a ride, though, since Chad couldn't pay him.

Before I climbed aboard his boat, I heard something being thrown overboard. I didn't see anything, but Chad said before getting stuck on shore, that they had left some fish out on the deck for bait for the sail up. He said things happen and to not freak out, because there were a few maggots on the deck. As I was climbing aboard, I looked down and saw the most revolting thing ever. It wasn't a few maggots, it was hundreds, maybe thousands of maggots crawling around on the floor of the deck! I had never seen anything like that in my life! It made my stomach churn and I had to look away. Chad found a dustpan and immediately was tossing them overboard. Fish instantly appeared and started devouring them. I kept my feet up on the bench somewhat watching, with disgust.

He said, "This is boat life hun, sometimes things like this happen." (RED FLAG). I understand if the food was left out for a few days, I get it, it doesn't mean I have to like it. I was very thankful none of them got into the cabin of the boat. It seemed like as soon as he cleared them off, they were multiplying and coming up from the drain hole. It took Chad a good while to clean them off.

After that mess was cleaned up and we went in the cabin, I saw the boat was loaded down and ready to set sail. He was still waiting for some batteries he ordered, though. His spirits seemed a lot better since I came down and he seemed to be even more motivated to get things rolling again. I was glad I was able to help in any way I could, and it made me feel good knowing I had that positive effect on him.

That night I gave Chad a surprise gift for his birthday, which came and went a few days earlier. It was a plaque I had ordered with our last names connected, and the date and coordinates of when and where we first met. He came up with our last names as our business name, for our Airbnb or our boat chartering business, and it flowed. He would occasionally bring it up, so I thought what a great gift to see it on a plaque. When he opened it, he just stared at it with his eyes watering. After he was able to compose himself, he said it was the best present he ever had. It was such a thoughtful gift and he loved it, so much so that he decided it would be the first thing everyone sees. He already knew exactly where he was going to hang it. I also got him a waterproof phone case since he was always dropping his phone in the water.

He said, "You really do love me!"

I said, "Yes I do."

"I love you too, Niki Rae," he replied.

We stayed up late talking. He talked about the sail up and I talked about all my upcoming events that I wanted him to be a part of. I wanted him to come to Alabama with me to meet my kids. Then I wanted him to go along with me to Epcot, and later fly with me to Seattle to meet my parents and family up there. In July I wanted him to accompany me to my daughter's wedding. I knew it sounded like a lot and quite overwhelming. The first thing was to get him to Alabama to meet my kids and get the approval for him to be my plus one at my daughter's wedding. All of this was happening in the next few months. If he really loved me, he would have to love my family too. I mentioned getting us a planner so we both could keep up with all the events and their details. After the wedding in July, and once all the events were over, we could then really start working on our business in St. Augustine. There was so much for us to look forward to. We fell asleep with our minds spinning from all the enjoyable things we were going to do together.

The next morning, after scooping up more maggots, Chad was out on the dinghy trying to get it working so he wouldn't have to depend on others to take him back and forth to shore. There was always something wrong, with never the right tools or equipment (RED FLAG). I imagined that it was hard trying to fix something out on the water. You couldn't just hop in your car and go to Lowes or Home Depot. It was a twenty minute dinghy ride to the docks and shore, neither an easy task nor a quick one. I started getting nervous knowing I needed to be getting on the road soon for my eight hour drive back to Julia's apartment to work the next day. I felt stuck, having to rely on someone else to get me to shore. I definitely would not want to be out on a mooring with a regular job. Having to use a dinghy to get back and forth was already a task that required some planning, and if I was trying to leave to go into work when the waves are high and choppy, I'd get wet. That's not something I would enjoy doing, walking into work smelling like the ocean. Then I'd be a nervous wreck if anything went wrong, either with the dinghy or the boat itself. We definitely needed to be parked at a marina where I could just walk off when needed. All these thoughts were racing through my head when Chad finally managed securing us a ride to shore.

On our way back to my truck, I was feeling pretty good and much better overall. I was pleased about my decision to drive down. I made Chad realize we were in this together, I wasn't going anywhere, and that we needed to support one another. That's how relationships work—you put more effort in because you're a team, not shut each other out during bad times. Chad also seemed to be in much better spirits than when I first saw him, which made me feel even more happy about showing up. When we made it to my truck, we said our I love you's, I loaded up and I got in, ready to head back to my current home. I looked out my window and there was an envelope with a parking ticket inside on my windshield. A $50.00 parking ticket. I was more than a little disappointed, mostly because Chad had said that was a good spot. While driving and we were on the phone,

I mentioned it to him, and he said to not worry because he would pay for it. He didn't seem to be as upset as I was (RED FLAG). I shrugged it off, thinking I would just add that to the marina bill, and he could transfer me some money when everything gets settled with his name change. I wasn't too worried about it at the moment. I felt like I had accomplished my mission of cheering him up. He was back to himself. It did cost me about $500.00 for the two nights, but that's what you do for the ones you love, right? (RED FLAG).

Chad was trying to keep me awake by texting me quite often when it started getting late on my drive home. After a while I stopped hearing from him, so I assumed he fell asleep. Thinking I wasn't going to hear from him the rest of the night, I texted, "I know you're probably asleep by now, but I just wanted to say sweet dreams, and that I love you."

Chad surprised me by replying, "I love you too sweetheart. And thank you for coming down. It meant a lot to me. It really did. I appreciate you."

"You're welcome, I knew you needed me, just like I needed you. It's a connection I've never felt before."

"I did need you. I needed your spirit to lift mine. I needed your soul to ease mine and bring it back to reality. I just needed to breathe you in, and all was well." Hearing those words made me melt.

After settling in at Julia's apartment that night, I told Chad how I had finally let my guard down and

113

was going along with these crazy feelings I had for him. It was scary and amazing at the same time. I also mentioned how I felt connected to the boat and that I felt like I belonged there. I also loved how he included me in everything. As much work as it would take us to get the boat in shape, I was ready for the challenge. I could see the end results in my head, and it looked fabulous. Chad had made me feel part of something that I had never been a part of before. We seemed to be in tune with each other. I often wondered if we were too much alike. Both free spirited with our minds always dreaming and planning and wanting to live life to the fullest. Would that hinder or facilitate us? I guess we would find out soon enough. I told him that I loved how we laugh at ourselves.

He replied, "Yea, we do laugh at ourselves. We are funny, lol. Get some sleep tonight sweetheart. I love you and I will see you in our dreams. Dream of me and I'll be right there with you. Oh, and you are always included. Why would I leave you out of anything? You go, we go."

I sent him two kissing emojis as my response.

He said, "Three kisses hun. Three. Always. Remember that for when we kiss hello and goodbye hun. And anytime in between."

I smiled to myself and sent three kissing emojis back before falling into a deep sleep.

Chapter 9

(I Love You)

I was back at work, and everything felt right with the world once again. I texted Chad telling him how much I hated leaving and I couldn't wait until we were together for good. He said he knew the feeling and that real soon we would be together.

I found a healthy food bowl place in St. Augustine that looked great for us to try and sent Chad the link. He told me good job sweetheart, that we would be a very healthy couple within a year, and I will love how his body shapes itself. He said he got lucky with good genes. I told him I got lucky too.

He said, "Yes you did hun. You're like the poster child for healthy living."

"We are going to look great in our 70's costumes for sure!"

"You already look amazing in yours," he replied.

I'm glad he liked me the way I was. Chad made me feel good about myself. I got excited thinking about going on bike rides, walks, hikes, and even to the gym with him. A partner that shared the same interests as me and wanted to grow together was always something that I had wanted in my life.

Thinking about the boat, I asked if the batteries came in yet. He said two out of the ten would be there the next day so he would cancel the other eight and only use two for on the way up. I had no idea he ordered ten batteries.

Chad said he spoke with Billy and said that Billy was still interested in doing the sail up with him, to his relief. They just needed to wait for the front that was coming in to go away first. Chad said the winds would change and the ride would be easier when the front passed. Billy just did the ride from Miami and said the waves were the length of Chad's sailboat.

Checking the planner I got for us, I told Chad that I hoped he could get up to St. Augustine by the next week. I wanted to take him to Alabama with me to meet my kids. He said he was working on it, but the winds were so bad at that time. He asked me to download "Wind finder for boaters" on my phone to keep track of the weather. I checked it out but couldn't really understand anything since I didn't know much about boats yet, so I never did download it.

At work I was feeling more and more defeated with COVID taking too many lives. It was getting depressing. Watching people die almost daily was not something I wanted to keep doing. My job seemed to be consisted of constantly taking care of sick people, getting attached and wanting to help in the best way possible, and then seeing or hearing that they died. I couldn't even count how many of my patients I had lost since the pandemic. I kept looking forward to getting out of the medical field to serve people in a positive and fun way. I knew I would probably work as needed in a hospital wherever Chad and I decided to live, but then I could control how often. Chad listened to my concerns and told me how sorry he was. He was thinking Airbnb with breakfast on our own yacht. Sailing charters would be our new path. I liked his thinking. I believed we would make that happen. We were both determined hard workers who loved people.

Chad sent me a photo of a yellow snapper he just caught off the boat. He said he was going to give it to Jerry (the homeless neighbor) because Jerry had no food. Once in a while he would let Jerry sleep on his boat when the weather was bad. Jerry's boat did not have a cover. I liked how Chad had a heart to help people out. Even when I had a hard day, he seemed to say the right things to cheer me up.

He'd say, "Just remember that I love you and your day will be over soon. Tomorrow's a brand new day."

I told him, "I'm so happy that you are in better spirits since I came down there to see you."

He said, "Yes hun, I am. I was down for a bit because of everything at once going against me. But you showing up like you did, that changed me from grumpy feeling shitty for myself for the moment....to knowing that you love me and everything will be alright. I just need to get there and start living instead of being here existing. But yes. You did fill me with smiles and warmth again I appreciate you for that. I haven't felt loved in a very, very long time, twenty five years or so, but you made sure I felt it again. I love you sweetheart."

"Aw, that is so sweet. And yes, I do love you, so very much. I'm finally letting out these feelings that I've been holding back because it seemed so fast and too good to be true. But knowing that you feel the same and love me back is helping me to release them. We are on the same page. I'm not sure that I have ever been on the same page with anyone before, maybe the same chapter, but never the same page. I thank you for that and for loving me back."

We chatted back and forth, and he was telling me about his friends who were fighting because the guy cheated on his wife. He said they basically lived a swinger's life, and you were bound to catch something at some point.

He said, "You never have to worry here sweetheart. I don't cheat, I do not look at other women at all like I look at you. They aren't even on the first step of the staircase that you're on top of. No worries about me. Seriously. You will see. I don't even go on lunch dates or out and about with any women at all. I have you."

I texted, "I know you don't, and I don't either. We have a beautiful thing we don't need anyone else. You're all I need."

He replied, "I know sweetheart. Kiss, kiss, kiss."

We would FaceTime quite often, and I would talk to him and anyone else who was visiting him on the boat. I liked how he included me with his friends, it was almost as if I was there. He had another new guy that was going to sail up with him, a guy named Milo. Milo had sailed before and planned on closing up his camp to leave Key West and travel back to New Mexico where he had a beautiful home full of art. Chad said when he mentioned sailing up, all of a sudden everyone wanted to ride along, like it was a cruise ship. Everyone had a story and wanted to contribute or leave Key West for one reason or another. He said he agreed with them for shits and giggles, but that it was really only going to be Milo and himself.

It was almost mid-April now and I was making another trip home to see the kids before Easter. I also needed to resolve an issue with my truck registration, renew my driver's license, go to the dentist and work on my taxes, along with fixing a few things around my house. While driving up I was sending Chad some videos of me singing to pass the time away. He said he loved them all and it made him happy to know I was a happy woman. I let him know that he was the one that made me happy.

A few hours went by, and Chad sent me a song called 'Without You' by Motley Crüe, saying that was his song to me. He just heard it, and it reminded him of us as he was singing it. It made my insides all mushy listening to it. I told him that he needed to be with me on this drive home.

He agreed and said, "I need to be there too sweetheart. My soul wants to be near yours. I'm not too far from you right now."

I felt like he truly was my soulmate. Our thoughts were so much alike.

The next day after running errands I decided to stop at the hospital and say hi to my friends and FaceTime Chad so he could meet them. It was important to me for everyone to know he was real, and that we were in a real relationship.

At the end of me introducing him to everyone and chatting through FaceTime, Chad was saying his goodbyes and said, "I love you sweetheart," while I was still on the phone.

I was not prepared for that and the only words I could muster up was, "You too."

I knew that was going to be a conversation later with him. I did love him, but to say it out loud in front of people was on a different level for me. It had been a while since those words left my mouth for a man, and I don't remember many times a man freely said that to me in front of people. It definitely threw me off guard and made me feel a little uncomfortable and embarrassed, my face even turned red. I knew my friends were concerned for me and thought we were taking things quite fast. I tried reassuring them that it was real, and I was happy. I let them know that I wasn't selling my home or doing anything drastic like that. Chad even had agreed for me to keep my home in a past conversation. That made them feel a little better.

As I was leaving, I noticed a text from Chad saying, "Oh, Love you. Lol. I can hear them busting your chops right now hun, lol."

He had thought it was funny that he made me feel uncomfortable in front of my friends. I was glad that he wasn't upset. I left my old hospital feeling a little lighter knowing we were okay, and my friends felt more okay with me and Chad.

I was busy the next few days. I texted and called Chad when I had time. He was also busy with working on the boat still. I wasn't sure what other things needed to be done before sailing, but I never did ask.

I sent him a picture of me in the dress I was planning on wearing to my daughter's wedding in July and his reply was, "Wow sweetheart, you look amazing. Where are you going today?"

"Nowhere, this is the dress I'm wearing for the wedding. I just got excited about it and wanted you to see it!" I told him.

He said, "I can't wait to go to the wedding just so I can be seen with you in that dress."

I thought how sweet, and I was hoping my daughter would be willing to let him be my plus one. I would hate to tell him he couldn't go, especially with us talking about it together so much. I wasn't going to worry about that just yet. Maybe after my daughter meets Chad, she would be okay with it. I never brought anyone to any of the functions my girls have had, so I knew it would be a big deal, and a little awkward. Even so, they are grown, and I've been divorced almost eight years. I would think that they would want me to be happy and to be with someone that I loved. I was ready to share my life with someone that had the same likes and interests as me. Someone who was proud to be with me, who supported me, lifted me up, and had a positive outlook on life. Someone who adored me, made me feel like I was number one with no competition, and loved me just as much as I loved them. I wanted someone who was ready to live life, not just exist in it.

Someone that wasn't scared to take chances and who was a little goofy and crazy. I found that someone in Chad. A life partner, a friend. He was that person. All I wanted was for my girls to see that.

After I had a very productive couple days at home, it was then time to drive back to Florida and get back to work. My next few days off I was planning a road trip to see Cookie and her family for Easter since I had nowhere else to go. They were my first adopted family, way back when I first had my twin daughters when we all lived in Florida. My ex-husband and I had no family anywhere nearby, but Cookie and her family moved in next to us and helped raise our girls while we both worked full time. It was always like going home when I saw them. Cookie lived down in Jupiter on the East Coast of Florida, and Chad would be sailing right by there, a few miles offshore though. Of course, that would also depend on if Chad finally was able to set sail by that point.

Chad and I had been video calling often and sometimes Julia would join us. And anyone on the boat helping Chad would drop in on his end as well. We were all able to meet each other that way. Julia was asking Chad about being a Ranger, so he sent me a video to show Julia of what it was like as a Ranger. We watched it that night and it clarified a few questions she had.

On April 16th, Chad gave me an update on what was going on. He took the old battery off the power in the boat and hooked everything up to the new battery. The boat was at full power again and the motor was running. He also removed a bunch of miscellaneous wires that didn't belong. He mentioned that Milo was impressed and called Chad an artist when it came to boats. He sent me pictures of him rewiring everything. I was glad that he was mechanically educated because I was not. I was proud of him for getting the boat right.

I asked if he was getting nervous.

He said, "No. Getting anxious. We are leaving tomorrow. Milo is getting his camp cleared. The Canadian is going for the ride then getting dropped off in Miami. Can't wait to see you. Breathe you in. That's all I need. I hope you're by Cookies house when we pass by. I'll make sure we come close to shore and possibly pick you ladies up for a bit. Depending on the weather and waves."

The Canadian was a girl named Stella, who was living free in Key West, saving up for a special surgery she was having in Miami after a car wreck. She was needing a ride to Miami and Chad offered for her to join them. She was more than happy to be a part of the adventure and to be able to make it to Miami at the same time. Julia and I had talked to her a few nights before on FaceTime. She seemed super sweet. I was glad there was more than just Chad and Milo sailing up. He also admitted that Jerry was going to ride up with them too. Jerry is a little off, but dependable, trustworthy, and a hard worker.

It definitely eased my mind to know there were four of them going now. So, all together it was Milo the artist, Jerry the homeless, and Stella the Canadian, all joining Chad on a cruise leaving Key West. Each one had their own personal reasons for a one way journey out in the Atlantic up the East coast of Florida.

After getting all caught up on what was happening on Chad's end, I was trying to explain to Chad all the plans for the next few months with my kids and how it seemed a little overwhelming to me. There seemed to be a year's worth of events happening in just three months, and I needed to be there for a good bit of them.

"What's going on the next few months? Everything is ok. No need to be overwhelmed sweetheart. I hope you're not having a second guess about me now hun. I'm doing everything here to leave to be with you." Chad replied.

124

I told him I wasn't having any second guesses and that I was sorry and shouldn't have even said anything, that he only needed to worry about getting up to me.

"No need to be sorry sweetheart." He told me.

"It's crazy how we can read each other, like how I was able to know that you needed me to come down to Key West to be with you and cheer you up." I told him.

"I'm thankful you did. I was losing it there for a minute. (Not us. Just reality because everything happened at once. Financially I took a huge hit and it hit me solid in the brain. So, you did help just by being you) You grounded me again. I'm almost ready to leave. Milo is parking his car and coming aboard. One last system check, and one more anchor to raise and we are setting sail."

"Yay! I'm so excited!" I replied.

"I'm coming hun, Milo is getting ice now."

It seemed that things were moving slow. When he said they were getting ready and about to leave, I was thinking any minute now. But hours would go by, and they would still be there (RED FLAG).

I told him to FaceTime me when they were moving.

He said, "Hun. We are leaving with sunrise. Still need to pull the mooring since it's coming with me. I paid ten grand for this gear (RED FLAG- more talk of money). Can't leave it. We voted and decided to leave first light. Call me anytime. Plus, with this mooring gear you and I can anchor off and leave the mooring and have a free space anywhere worldwide. I bought all the gear already. Reason being hun. My mooring lines wrapped around a few chains of someone else who dragged. It's of course a cluster down there. But we are all ready to sail so that's all that's keeping us. That's it. We are shoving off first light. So about nineish actually. To be safe."

I told him that would be about the same time I would be leaving to go to Cookie's house for Easter.

Easter came and went with no sailing from Chad. I was starting to wonder if him sailing up would ever be a reality. I understood how winds could be a factor, but that had been going on for quite some time now. I couldn't explain how frustrated I was getting. All my friends and family kept asking when he was setting sail. It was beginning to be embarrassing. I stopped saying anything to them. It seemed at that point I would be lucky if he was in St. Augustine before July. Crossing my fingers, I held my breath and tried to stay positive.

Chapter 10

(Sailing)

Finally, on April 18th, they set sail! They pulled up the anchor and out to sea they went! For real this time! I was ecstatic! I was also able to FaceTime them on the start of their journey. It felt like I was there with them because they all made me feel included. The weather was beautiful, and everything was going as planned. It was a great feeling knowing that this guy was wild enough about me to leave Key West and sail up to St. Augustine, all for me. That was huge in my book.

As we were FaceTiming, Chad mentioned a huge storm ahead and that he was going to have to go and make sure everything was secure. We said our "I love you's" and hung up.

I was a nervous wreck not being able to talk to him and wondering where they were and how they were doing. And how far out was that storm? At that moment I felt helpless.

It wasn't until the next day, April 19th, that I was finally able to FaceTime Chad. He looked terrible! He was lying down inside the boat, pale, and he could hardly move. He said he went down to open the engine room to check on something and got hit with a blast of carbon monoxide. He was sick instantly. I could tell he was slightly confused, and he mentioned having a headache and some chills. His words were jumbled and seemed to be talking crazy. He kept saying how sorry he was that he was sick and might not be able to continue the journey to be with me. He was telling me how sorry he was for letting me down, that he was trying his best to be with me. Then he would repeat everything he just said.

I told him to get outside and to breathe in some fresh air. He said he could hardly move and that he had chills. I didn't care, I told him he needed to get outside, that carbon monoxide poisoning was no joke. He couldn't talk long for not feeling well, so we hung up. I felt so bad.

A few hours went by, and he texted, "We can stay on the air mattress at Julia's place and pay half of the rent for the next twelve weeks hun. That's if I bring the boat back to Key West and anchor it off and come up North. Or I can continue this voyage. You let me know what you want me to do. I can put the boat in Key West, and we can move onto her as soon as you're done there. Or I can continue this voyage and see what happens. Everyone onboard is concerned for me. Let me know what you want me to do sweetheart. I just want to be with you."

"Oh hun, I know you're not feeling well right now and you just want to be with me. I want nothing more than to be with you too. Let's sleep on it and talk about it in the morning. We will make it work. I love you and I just want you feeling better. And if we rent it's about $1600 to $1700 a month. I have no problem with that as long as you pay half." I replied.

The next night came with no word from Chad. I was getting so worried for him knowing he was sick with carbon monoxide poisoning, and they were out in the ocean with a storm in the forecast.

I was texting him that I was looking up apartments since Julia was not supposed to have anyone live with her, she was only letting me stay there because it was temporary. I told him it was hard finding a place for only three months. He still wasn't responding.

It had been two days since they set sail. He finally answered the morning of April 20th, with a "no" when I asked him if he'd been keeping any fluids down. I was so relieved that I heard from him, even if it was only a two letter word. I wanted to know more, but at least he answered, and it reassured me that he was alive. I was thinking the worst, wondering if he passed out, got air lifted to a hospital, etc.

The day passed by without any more contact with Chad. He still needed to be very careful out at sea with being hit by the carbon monoxide. I was on edge wondering what was happening out there. He was talking about a storm coming. I couldn't imagine being sick and then having to deal with a storm on top of that.

It was in the afternoon when Chad texted saying they may turn back. They hit a major storm and had already lost one of the two dinghy's that they had. He said the boat was getting beat up really bad.

I texted back telling him to do what he needed to do, that his health was the most important thing to think about at that moment.

Five hours went by, and I finally was able to talk to Chad on the phone. With barely any reception, I tried my best to keep up with what he was saying. He was telling me that he was sorry, and he didn't blame me if I didn't want to see him anymore. He said he was trying to sail the boat up, but with the carbon monoxide poisoning and the storm, everything got out of control, and it failed him. He said he wasn't sure what they were going to do, that the storm was beating them all up with ten foot swells and they were all holding on for dear life. He said all that he was thinking about was me, that I was keeping him breathing. He added how he had worked so hard to make this happen, and it was a disaster, and he was so sorry, but to not forget that he loved me. Then the phone died.

I tried reassuring him through text that I still loved him, and it wasn't his fault what was happening. And whatever he decided was okay with me. He really just needed to see a doctor.

Sleep did not happen for me that night, I was too busy worrying about what was happening with them out at sea during a storm.

Chad finally answered the phone the next morning, and it was now April 21st. Chad was full of adrenaline and told me the whole story. They hit a major storm, and it tore up the outside of the boat.

130

Chad said he was outside helping Milo and Jerry while Stella stayed inside. They all took turns throwing up with the heavy rocking. The boat was rocking with the high waves and the mast (the tall pole that holds the sails in place) would touch the water each time, making it feel like it was going to tip over, from one side to the next. The rain was pounding down on them making it hard to see. They were holding on with their lives. Then the rudder (a rudder steers the boat) broke loose at some point and they were not able to steer the boat. He said the boat turned on its own as if it was alive, and it was headed out to sea away from land. He really thought he was going to die. He said the only thing he was thinking about was me and how he failed me. Before giving up they sent off a flair to get help. They were all scared and really thought they might go down with the boat and depart their lives right there in the ocean. None of them could remember how long it was before the Coast Guard found them and towed them to a mooring ball outside of a marina. There were no slips available at any marinas at that time. They were all just happy to be alive. The only way then to get to shore was with Jerry's kayak. Their journey landed them in Marathon Key, which was just an hour North of Key West.

A few hours later, Chad was telling me I needed to call the marina that they were staying at to pay for the mooring ball since he left all his credit cards on his bike (RED FLAG). He told me he left them there because he heard that one of the passengers had sticky fingers and he wanted to be safe. I never had time to call the marina, nor did I hear anything more about it.

131

A little while later he asked, "Can we move to Alabama for a while? I need a break. I'm ready to have a breakdown. Too much stress with this boat. I need a week at least away from her."

I told him that I still had eleven more weeks at my job, and that we needed to talk about all of that if that's what he really wanted.

He replied, "Jerry said he would watch the boat for me while I take a sabbatical. Whew. I'm so sorry sweetheart. I didn't mean to let you down. I tried to get there. Surprise storm destroyed the boat. Should I sell her for fifty? Or should we keep her and refurbish her. Think about it. We can talk about it face to face. It's an option. Whatever you want sweetheart. I just want to be with you."

"That's your call," I said, "but maybe it's for the best and then we can look for something together. Start fresh. You could buy a motor home and I could take a travel assignment somewhere and we could explore the area we land at. We could head out West and I could show you around where I grew up in Oregon. Then we could come back to Florida and find us a spot on the beach. We could then Airbnb the motor home out."

"Ok sweetheart. We will talk, that sounds nice. Traveling the U.S. with you in a motor home. See everything. Then do Airbnb. I'll be getting a job as well wherever we wind up with your work. I took a major hit with the boat sweetheart. Starting fresh may be our solution. Let me think on it. I know you've been jealous of the boat. Joking."

Our brains were in overdrive thinking about what to do next. The first thing I did was cancel the marina in St. Augustine. I had already paid for two months; it was on a monthly payment plan. The dock master was a little upset, but he understood. He would not have any problem renting the slip out.

There was a lot to think about. My job was just temporary right now, but if we were serious about starting over, we really had to think about where we would be staying, and for how long. Would we sell the boat or fix it up? Would we get a motor home together, and what about my house? The boat was Chad's home, and now his home was damaged, along with his ego. It did sound like he needed some time away. That made me start thinking of my next few days off that I could take Chad to Alabama with me so he could meet my kids. That meant that I'd have to drive to Marathon Key to pick him up. My mind was non-stop racing. I really wanted to make this work.

The next morning Chad was in a little bit of a panic since Stella's credit card was not going through to pay for the towing fee. Chad wanted me to pay with my card and said he would pay me back (RED FLAG). Of course, I believed him, and I did pay for it, but my heart skipped a beat when I found out it was $2,145.50. Wow, he was starting to owe me quite a bit of money. I was thinking I really needed to keep track of it all so he would know how much to repay me, so I started to keep all the receipts and papers in a folder.

It was in the afternoon when he texted, "Ok. So, I kicked the Canadian off the boat. Her man came and picked her up. Milo and Jerry are still here for a few more days, until I'm able to get to Key West. Which means I have to get the dinghy going tomorrow. I think I need an impeller for her though. $125 at the parts store. Easy fix. I'll get it done. Lol."

If he was serious about us staying in an apartment near my job, I told him that he'd have to pay half, and we needed to act soon. I also mentioned that I would be taking him to my home in Alabama soon. He never really said much about any of that, he just listened (RED FLAG).

A little later that day, when I was trying to have some alone time to think, I sat on the porch at Julia's apartment. What a mess Chad and I got ourselves into. Pretty soon my thoughts got interrupted by the neighbors. They were heavy into a fight about their dog. Apparently, the dog shit all over inside their vehicle. It seemed a little excessive to me to have a major fight over, but it was entertaining, and I decided to listen in. I told Chad about it.

He said, "That's not going to be you and I hun. We are better than that. I know you love me. I hope you know I love you. Together we won't be that couple that you just saw. We will be the couple others envy."

I was glad he didn't want to fight. I'm not a fighter either. We were going make a great team and I was looking forward to all of it. It was a dream for both of us to finally be together and be out as a couple. We were trying really hard to turn that dream into our reality.

Later in the day he texted, "I have a friend coming to get me on Saturday to take me to town to go get my bike. I left my things on my bike because I didn't trust the Canadian. Supposedly she has sticky fingers. Which come to find out she does. She took the hundred and fifty I had in my change jar before she left. It was in the V berth where she slept. Just realized that five minutes ago."

"I can't believe she took all of your change," I replied.

"It was bills. Not change. She left the pennies. I had maybe forty in quarters. This is why I left my important info on my bike. I knew I was going to get my bike with you. So, it didn't matter to me. Now I wish I would've taken my stuff," he replied.

I felt bad that everything was going wrong for him. He was even asking me if I was mad at him that he didn't make it up. I told him that I wasn't mad, I was a little sad that my vision of us on the boat in St. Augustine wasn't going to happen. I said it's my own fault for getting too excited over things, and that I should have known better.

He said, "No hun. Not your fault. Don't think that please. I was more than excited to go. I just hit a surprise storm out there and wound up Adrift. We can't predict the weather. I was coming up there hun. So, I'll list the boat and if and when she sells, I will buy you something nice. A ring? I'll start looking for an RV. Maybe one to build up to your specs."

All I said back to that was, "Let's get you better, first."

"Yes dear. I need some sleep sweetheart. I did watch on the last night and then the lines snapped. That's when I realized I had no rudder. The boat took us out to sea and guided me away from the coral reefs. This was a hell of a twenty four hours. All while I felt like shit and puking."

I told him it was hard on me too, the waiting and wondering. It was time we both needed to get some mental rest. It was all very draining.

He added, "Honestly, this is a kick in the pants for me. But I thought about you the whole time I was out there. You were my rock out there. You and I will do the wood on this boat and then you and I can get good money for her sweetheart. I'm probably still going to have her in eleven weeks. We can still live the marina life in the Keys till she sells. Or whatever you want to do. I do want to go to Alabama. Get some rest. Dream of me and I'll be right there with you. We didn't lose the fight sweetheart. Just wounded a little. We don't talk about the pain. Just lick the wounds and soldier up. I'll get the boat better than she was before. She will be a happy fat ass again."

I was too overtired to reply, and it was time for some much needed rest, especially since I had to work the next day.

It was the morning of April 23rd, five days after they left Key West and they were still out on a mooring ball waiting for a slip to open up. We FaceTimed while I walked from the parking garage to the hospital. It was good to see Chad feeling better and more like himself. We talked about staying in Marathon while fixing the boat up. They had a little hospital there that I was hoping I might could get a job at. I could probably even ride my bike to work. Marathon seemed like a nice little town and only one hour from Key West. I was starting to like the idea more and more. Some things don't go as planned, but you can always accommodate the new arrangements. I try to be positive and make the best of every situation. There's no need to worry or stress yourself to death. It will only lead to more damage. In my book, if you stress and worry too much about what's to come, it just means you suffer twice. I try to live by those words, even though I can't help but to stress at times.

I had slept pretty well the night before, so I was in a positive mood and ready for the day. After hanging up with Chad he texted, "It was nice seeing you smile this morning. It uplifted my spirits a bunch. You are so beautiful sweetheart."

A few minutes later I got another text from him saying, "I just spoke to the dinghy dock master. When I'm able to get into a dock, I'll need to call you again sweetheart."

Since he left all his credit cards and money on his bike, he needed me to pay for the mooring ball once again (RED FLAG). I wasn't sure how I felt about that, I had already been covering up for him financially, more so than I had planned. He mentioned his friend taking him to go get his bike, so why wasn't that happening? I never was one to ask questions, I don't know why, but I didn't start there. Instead, I just got so confused and frustrated with what was going on down there. It appeared that everything was in slow motion, and nobody ever was in a hurry to do anything. I knew that was the way it was on the islands, and I was actually looking forward to that being me one day. But it was very hard to comprehend at the moment when your current lifestyle revolved around time limits, like my full time job that you have certain hours you punch in and out and will get a tardy if you're late. I was learning to be patient, and that it would all work out. It wasn't fun, though.

In the meantime, I was looking forward to taking care of a few of the patients at the hospital. After arriving in the unit I'd been working at, I checked my charts and those patients weren't there. When I asked around to see if they got discharged, I learned they passed away. I had a hard time with that information since I had gotten close to them. I love working with people and helping them, I just don't like them dying on me. I was looking forward to working with healthy people in the future. I was texting Chad what a bad morning I was having, and I needed to talk to someone.

"I'm sorry sweetheart. Everything will be ok. Just remember I love you," Chad responded, with kisses and heart emojis.

He was always trying to make me feel better and knew what to say. The day was hard, but I managed to get through it.

Chad never did mention the fee for the mooring ball again. I had my credit card handy just in case but was thankful I didn't have to use it.

The next day, that same credit card was credited the $2,145.50 that was charged for the towing fee. I was guessing that Stella's (the Canadian) card went through after all. I was so relieved, but I felt bad for Stella. I let Chad know and he said he didn't feel bad for her at all because she had dropped some silverware that was worth a lot of money from his family into the ocean and that her boyfriend had broken the handle to the toilet also. He said now they were even.

Stella was so nice to me when we were chatting on FaceTime with Chad while they were sailing up. She didn't seem like the kind of person who would steal money or throw nice things in the ocean. But I only had his word to go by. I wasn't there to witness any of it.

I had a few days off and I was planning on driving to Marathon to pick Chad up and bring him back to Alabama to meet my kids. I would stay the night on the boat with him, then we would head back up for a long drive home. My friend Selena had never been to the Keys and asked if she could ride with me. It would definitely make the ride more enjoyable, so I invited her along.

While waiting for the day to pass, I was looking up houses in Marathon that we could possibly buy and rent out. I mentioned it to Chad and added how they were so expensive.

He answered, "Let's get the boat fixed...then decide where we want to move to sweetheart. We can go anywhere. I'd like to be closer to your family actually. I want them to be a part of our lives on a regular and not just once a year etc. We will have plenty of time to talk this out sweetheart."

"Sounds perfect to me. I would love to be near the kids."

I filled him in on Selena riding down with me.

"Ok sweetheart. No problem. Totally ok with that. Milo is leaving tomorrow. Jerry is going to his boat tomorrow then coming back on our boat with us. So, it will be the four of us on our boat. BBQ time. Just be. The four of us. I love you hun. Just saying. Oh, and let Selena know that the boat is filthy, she may need a tetanus shot."

It was almost a week since they set sail and have been stranded out on the water. I couldn't imagine what it looked like on the inside of the boat by this time. I was also wondering if any of them had even showered anytime since then. I guess we would find out soon enough.

The next morning Selena and I would be off to Marathon Key.

Chapter 11

(Marathon)

It was April 25th, and Selena and I were on our way to the Keys to pick up Chad. Selena slept most of the way but enjoyed the scenery from Miami on into the Keys. We were getting close, and Chad was telling us they were getting towed into the marina and once again needed my credit card to pay for the slip (RED FLAG). He sent me the phone number to the marina for me to call and pay over the phone. I pulled over to call them. They were expecting my call and said it was going to be $1,704.10. $284.02 was prorated for April, and May's rent was going to be $1,420.08, which would be a recurring monthly payment. It definitely was not cheap to live in the Keys, even on a boat, I was quickly finding out. I was looking forward to Chad's bank to finally get all his paperwork straightened out so he could get to his money. I didn't mind helping out, but I was not one to pay interest on my credit cards, so I would need to get the money back to pay them off before a payment was due. Chad just made it through a major ordeal with the carbon monoxide poisoning, while in a storm, and then having to live out on a mooring ball for almost a week, so I hated to mention money right away. Plus, when he did mention money, it was always how he wasn't used to spending that much and he was stressed because of it, so it kind of made me feel like I shouldn't bring it up much anyway (RED FLAG).

Chad was getting towed in as we were driving. He said they should be there shortly, and he couldn't wait to see us. He let me know what slip they were being towed into so we could meet them there.

Selena and I finally made it to the marina and started checking out the place right away. It was a beautiful facility that included a restaurant, laundry room, bathrooms, a little convenience store, and a pool. The area was very clean, charming, and quaint. There were a lot of fabulous boats, sailboats, and yachts, and all of them would be our neighbors. I couldn't believe I would actually be living there. I was totally picturing it: my new life with Chad on the marina slip while I'm working part time as a respiratory therapist, or a bus driver for a local school. Then coming home to my beautiful boat and wonderful husband (if we did get married), while watching the sunrises and sunsets and having boat parties all the time. Maybe even learn yoga and teach a class on the boat with mimosas. It seemed like a dream come true.

Since Selena and I got there before Chad did, we walked the docks and looked for our slip. It was next to a young couple on a more modern sailboat. We had a few minutes to kill so we walked to the end of the dock to soak up the scenery. It was such a beautiful day with clear skies and a nice breeze. Before the boat turned the corner being towed in, we noticed a couple dolphins playing in the water. That would soon be my life. It was thrilling to think about, and definitely a dream I've been waiting on.

144

We could see Chad and Jerry on the boat, and we all waved at each other. The neighbors were out and willing to help tie up the boat. It wasn't easy without a rudder to steer, so we all had to pitch in and hold on to the ropes to help get the boat into its spot. The boat was heavy and big, and if you didn't watch out or pay attention, it would pull you right into the water with her. She was a sturdy, solid vessel. One of the neighbors helping came over, introduced herself to me as Bailey and helped me tie the boat off from my rope. I told her that I had no idea how to even do that, but I was willing to learn. She said she just learned herself. Her and her boyfriend Derrick met in Hawaii, but she was from California and had no history of boating. She told me about their YouTube channel of their adventures together. I told her that's what Chad and I wanted to do. She said it was easy and she would teach me. We exchanged numbers and we were both excited to be neighbors soon. I could picture us hanging out quite often, and I was already feeling like I fit in.

As soon as Chad got off the boat, I went over to him, and we hugged for what seemed like fifteen minutes. It was so great to see him well and alive. He told me how much he had missed me and thought about me the whole time. He added how he was so sorry he let me down. I reassured him it was all good and that we were meant to be in Marathon.

Jerry was also excited to see me and to meet Selena. After all the introductions, Jerry and Chad helped transport the blankets, pillows, some clothes, and kitchen stuff from my truck onto the boat. I felt a little giddy unpacking some of my stuff onto my soon-to-be new home!

It was a perfect day out, so we all did some relaxing on the boat before our quick trip to Key West to get Chad's cards he left on his bike. After the guys showered, Selena and I listened to them tell us about the storm they were in, and how they really thought they weren't going to make it. They said it was just like in the movies, with big choppy waves rocking the boat and the rain coming down where you could barely see in front of you. Jerry told the story of how sick Chad was. Chad said he was trying to help up on the deck and accidentally threw up on Jerry during the storm. We had some good laughs with that one. Neither one of them had went through anything like that ever. They had one hell of a week, and one real fine story to tell. Then after all that, they landed only one hour north of where they started. That made for another good laugh.

It was getting late, and I wanted us to get going to Key West. We had an early morning the next day to head up North. Jerry wanted to stay back, so Chad, Selena, and myself took off to Key West. Selena was excited to see the town. We made it to Harpoon Harry's where Chad left his bike, and Selena and I waited at the truck for Chad to retrieve his credit cards. He came back a minute later extremely upset. Apparently, someone broke into his bike while he was gone and took everything (RED FLAG). He said he parked it there because of the cameras everywhere, and he would have to talk to the owner of Harpoon Harry's to look at the footage on the camera. Chad

had all of his personal cards on the bike and even something for me. I felt bad for him. He would not have the time to go talk to the owner of Harpoon Harry's or to go to the bank until we got back from going up North. I knew at that point I would be paying for our trip back up to Alabama (RED FLAG). It was mainly gas and food, so that was okay with me. As long as he was able to go with me to see my daughters, I was happy with it.

There was nothing we could do at that point about his credit cards or cameras, so Chad and I decided to show Selena what Key West was all about and go to Mallory square for the sunset festival. After sightseeing and looking for a parking spot, we missed the sunset, but we were able to enjoy all the festivities, and the colors of the sky were astonishing even though the sun had already set. Chad and I were holding hands, walking along the water when we turned around to tell Selena something, and she was gone. We looked all around and started to get a little worried until we found her watching a magic show. We laughed at how we felt like she was our kid, having to keep up with her. She was almost thirty years younger than me, so she very well could have been my daughter. I was happy to see her enjoying herself. We all agreed it was time to get some food and get back to the boat for some sleep before our fifteen hour drive the next day.

It was an hour drive from Key West back to Marathon where the boat was. On our way back we stopped at a Publix for me to buy food for everyone. We carried it all back to the boat to share with Jerry, who was waiting and starving. After eating, we loaded up the truck with all of the clothes and blankets from the boat that needed washing, which was basically everything except the fresh blankets I had brought down. Chad also wanted to bring up this brain coral he said he found on Wisteria Island. It was beautiful. I couldn't believe he found it. I wasn't even sure if you were supposed to have coral. It was already dead, so I guess it was okay.

We settled in for the night. Jerry was going to sleep outside on the side of the boat, Selena wanted to sleep on the deck under the canopy, and Chad and I were going to sleep in the v-berth (the front of the boat). We all fell asleep pretty quickly since everyone was spent from the day. Around one in the morning a downpour woke us all up. I thought about Jerry and Selena and jumped up to help zip up the sides of the canopy. Jerry was outside getting soaked zipping up all the sides he could. Selena was under a blanket but getting rained on. I told her to get inside. I told Jerry to come inside also, but he refused. He said he would rather sleep outside where he was the most comfortable. I reckon living on a boat with no shelter became comfortable to Jerry.

There were a few tears in the canopy and water was leaking around a couple of the windows. The storm they went through did some damage. Nothing that couldn't be fixed, though. We all slept a few more hours before it was time to get on the road.

We left Jerry on the boat with the remainder of the food from the night before, and Chad said there was enough food still in the cabinets that Jerry would be fine while we were gone. Jerry wanted to stay on the boat and keep an eye on it for us. We couldn't say no, especially when he kept insisting. After a little bit of back-and-forth, double and triple checking, that's what he wanted to do, so we said, okay. The boat probably needed a babysitter, anyway, with how much bad luck it was getting.

Our drive up North seemed to take forever. Chad insisted on driving, but I found out soon enough he was the slowest driver I've ever seen, even on the interstates. I told him to use the cruise control, but he refused. I gave up on "backseat driving" and tried not to get too focused on how slow we were going. While on the road, Selena was questioning Chad about when he was overseas in the military. He was answering each question, but I could tell he was getting a little nervous, and his eyes started watering. I told her we needed to change the subject. He thanked me and said he was going to have to pull over and walk it off if she kept asking. I knew he didn't like talking about his time overseas, especially in that depth.

We finally made it to Gainesville, which should have only taken seven hours, but as slow as Chad was driving and the multiple stops we made, it took about nine hours. We dropped off Selena at her car, and it was time for us to refresh before we hit the road again. Everyone was happy to get out of the truck for a much needed break and stretch. It was another eight hours to Alabama but would turn into ten hours if I let Chad drive the whole way. I was definitely not going to let that happen. I was ready to get to my house in Alabama sooner than later. That was going to be the longest trip for myself and Red, driving in one day! From almost the southernmost point in Florida (Marathon) to North Alabama (Madison).

During our drive, we stopped to get gas and coffee at Buc-ee's. The cashier did not say "Welcome to Buc-ee's" when we arrived like they usually do. While paying for our coffee, we told her that when the next customers came in, we wanted to hear her say "Welcome to Buc-ee's" and that we would help. When a couple walked in, the cashier and all of us in line welcomed them to Buc-ee's. Everyone was laughing and the couple looked so confused. I think everyone was delirious because it was about one or two in the morning. We laughed so hard that tears were running down our faces. It was so nice and refreshing to know that even a mundane task like getting coffee in the middle of the night can be entertaining, as long as you're with the right person.

A different couple in line behind us was buying a frisbee and soccer ball. After Chad and I bought our coffee, we sat on the tailgate of Red, and joked about having a soccer game against the North and the South. We laughed about that too. That's what life is about: having fun, and we definitely had fun together. Everything seemed so easy for us. We finished our coffee and was ready to get back on the road.

Before heading out, we had to get our picture with Buc-ee, and we joked at how it would be funny to have a bunch of empty beer cans and cigarettes at the bottom of his feet for when all the morning people arrived. It would let everyone know how much of a party animal Buc-ee really was. Again, we just laughed until our stomachs hurt. Who knew you could be so amused at a gas station in the middle of the night!

As we were getting closer to my home, the more excited I was getting about bringing Chad into my world. I was a little disappointed that it was early in the morning and still dark when we got there. I was hoping we could do a few things I had mentally planned, but that wasn't going to happen. We were so exhausted that we went right to sleep as soon as we entered the house anyways.

Chapter 12

(Alabama)

The next morning after a good night's sleep, Chad was up on a ladder cleaning out my gutters while I started laundry and breakfast. Our plans were to watch my grandson a little bit and have the kids come over in the afternoon for dinner and to meet Chad.

When picking up my grandson, he recognized Chad right away from us FaceTiming him. They got along great, all of Chad's attention was then on my grandson. It was adorable. After picking up my grandson, we went to Publix to pick up food for an Italian dinner that Chad was wanting to make for everyone. Before starting dinner, Chad decided to show my grandson how to pressure wash my driveway. The sight gave me butterflies and I thought my grandson looked so funny, with him being only three years old with a pressure washer. I was impressed by how Chad was with my grandson. He was so patient and wanted to show my grandson how to do everything. There were times it felt like I was watching two kids instead of one. I was also very pleased that Chad actually wanted to help out with my cleaning chores I fell behind on. We cleaned the gutters, the driveway, and even had my tiny backyard all looking a lot better than I remember leaving it.

It was time to start the chicken parmesan, stuffed peppers, and salad. Chad was finally showing me his skills in the kitchen. I tried to help by cleaning up after him, but he did not want me in the kitchen with him. He told me that all I needed to do was to look pretty with a glass of wine while watching. I had no problem with that. While I was drinking my glass of wine, I was surprised at how Chad knew his way around the kitchen. There's nothing sexier than watching a man cook for you. My grandson was curious about Chad and appeared in the kitchen watching. Chad got down on his level and explained to him that the oven was hot and no matter what, you did not go near it. Chad was really good with kids. Then, while cooking the chicken on the stove, and pre-heating the oven to cook the bread, everything decided to stop working.

I tried resetting the circuit breaker, but it would not keep the stove and oven on at the same time. Chad had to finish cooking the chicken on the grill and I had to go to the neighbors to finish cooking the bread. When I came back, one of my daughters had already shown up. I noticed Chad looked a little frazzled and embarrassed that the stove quit on him, and he had to cook a different way than he planned. The dinner still turned out great, and I knew he was really trying his best to impress my kids. He kept apologizing for the inconvenience and he was hoping it was okay. It was more than okay; everything turned out perfect and delicious. I never knew how good of a cook Chad was until that day. I was a lucky woman. The girls didn't say anything, but I felt like it went well and that they approved.

Eventually we figured out that we had too much going on, literally. The laundry, lights, and stove were all connected to the same circuit. I had forgotten I was doing laundry, with one load in the washer and another in the dryer, both going while we had the oven and stovetop on. Next time we would not be doing laundry at the same time as cooking. It took a little bit longer than expected to finish up the loads of laundry we had.

Later that evening we weighed the brain coral he brought to keep at my house and looked up how much it was worth. He showed me and one of my daughters that it was worth $7,800.00 on eBay. We talked about making it into a table somehow and how cool that would look in our future houseboat.

Chad also thought about how we could sell aquariums with stands that we could make out of driftwood. If we stayed in Alabama, he could go to Key West once a month to get the driftwood from Wisteria Island, along with any other finds we could use in the tables or aquariums. All I thought about was how we couldn't leave the boat in the Keys unattended, but I also knew he was just brainstorming like I did. I know when my thoughts go that crazy, I usually let them go until they run out, or someone has to rein me in, or have someone humor me with my ideas. It hurt when someone would shut my ideas down, even if they were crazy. The point of me thinking about them was that they were ideas that I needed to figure out on my own, whether they would work or not. I didn't mind suggestions at all, but it was the instant rejection that stabbed me like a knife. I knew how that felt, so I didn't want to ruin his train of thoughts either, so I just listened to them. Usually, it was my mind all over the place. I wasn't used to being with someone that was so similar to me. It was exciting, but also a little apprehensive and overwhelming at times.

After finishing and sorting some of the laundry, Chad and I decided to keep some of his clothes at my house. We decided we would both be back for Mother's Day and then all of July. With him keeping some clothes at my house, he wouldn't have to bring as many clothes next time. I had the laundry still going since it seemed like he brought up everything he had. It felt like I finished a dozen loads, and there were still even more left! We would have to finish the rest of his laundry when we returned in two weeks. There's only so much you can do in a couple days. It was too short of a trip to do much of anything, but a much needed one for Chad to meet two out of three of my girls.

It was an eight hour trip back to Gainesville where I worked. We took our time, taking turns driving. Every time Chad drove, he was slower than molasses, like he had no cares in the world. I had cares, like a job I needed to be at the next morning. It was late when we finally arrived, so Chad stayed the night with me in the apartment. I decided to let him take Red back to Marathon the next morning to the boat for the week. The plan was for him to come back up to get me so we can drive together back up to Alabama for Mother's Day. Since Julia had just bought a second car, I really didn't need my own vehicle at that time. I could either borrow Julia's second car or ride with her to work. That was the beauty of having a roommate and working most shifts together. Before Chad left, I filled Red up with gas and gave him one hundred dollars to make sure he made it to Marathon, since he had no money (RED FLAG).

I was sure that this time he would go to his bank and get all of his accounts taken care of during the week. When that was all settled, he would have his own money to get gas to drive back up to me. Plus, he would be able to send over at least part of the money that he owed me through a money transfer app. After that, we could start talking about fixing up the boat and brainstorming on business opportunities. There should be plenty of ways to make some money living in the Keys. Our future with each other was about to get real. After my daughter starts her new life of being married in July, Chad and I would be starting our new lives together in August. We had so much to look forward to, and I was savoring all of it.

Chapter 13

(Tickets)

It was April 29th, and I went back to work while Chad drove my truck to Marathon. Everyone at work said I was glowing once again. They knew I had taken Chad to my home to meet my kids, although he still had one more to meet over Mother's Day. I was hoping that particular meeting would go just as well as the last one did.

Chad sent me a text with the song Hooked on a Feeling by Blue Swede and said, "This is what I sang fifty times on the way home because of you. This is how you make me feel."

"Aw, you really do know how to make me smile!"

"You're my girl sweetheart. And I do love you. You make sure I feel loved, and I know that. I am grateful for you loving me. I will do everything I can to make sure you know that I love you as well."

I cherished hearing him say things like that to me. It always put my mind to rest.

That afternoon when he arrived at the boat, Chad let me know the neighbors Bailey and Derrick told him to tell me hello. I thought that was so sweet of them. He also said that Sloppy Joe's wanted him to work but he refused. He said he needed to stay on the boat to start fixing it up. I thought that was a good thing, he did need to get started on fixing it up.

The next morning, he texted me telling me to have a wonderful day and that he loved me. I was so busy that I didn't see it for a while, but when I did it made me smile. Later that day I asked him how his day was going.

He replied, "It's going. I think I got used to freezing. I'm burning up now. Lol. I came below in the shade because the sun is relentless. Besides that, I'm good. Moving forward with fixing the boat back up. Have the whole back room torn apart. Got rid of all the junk. Have to do another load of trash later consisting of stuff not needed. Going to wash the boat down when the sun isn't over head tonight. I think we should look for a nicer marina. Not just a transient one like this one. There are better marinas than this one around. I realize this is a transient one. People come and go. Not live aboard who stay and form a community. Different."

I told him we would find the right one for us, that it's like looking for the right church in Alabama. When I first moved to northern Alabama, I noticed a lot of churches around and it seemed like people didn't ask "if" you go to church, but "where."

He said, "Oh hun.... I would probably catch fire if I walked into a church again."

I told him he would not and that I was just saying that because there's a lot of marinas around in Florida, just like there's a lot of churches in Alabama.

"I know what you were saying. Lol. I'm going topside to help Jerry. He got himself a job cleaning some guy's hull. Lol."

"Oh, good for Jerry! That's great" I responded.

"They watched him cleaning the stainless on the boat and offered him a quick cash job. They just got back. Have a wonderful afternoon sweetheart. We will talk tonight. Call me when you get home or done. I would go to Church again for you if that's your family's thing. Just saying."

I wasn't implying that we go to church, but that was sweet of him to say he would go with me. That was important to know. It also reassured me that he was willing to do whatever I wanted in order to make me happy, which in itself made me happy.

It was May 1st, and I received a text from Chad saying, "Hi hun, I hope you're having a good day. I just got a call from the other marina I was at. Can you call me please. I need to pay for the ball I was on. Like eighty-eight bucks for four days. Forgot about it. Went to Key West thinking it was Monday to the bank and it was closed. It's Sunday. I went to the other marina to talk to them, and they were very rude. They said if I don't pay the eighty-eight today that they are going to put a lien on my boat. For eighty-eight bucks? Fuk. I just filled the truck up with the fuel and went shopping for food just now. Then I went to the marina like an idiot after that. I should've gone before. They wouldn't take sixty cash as a down till tomorrow when I can show my face at a bank with my bank guy and reopen my account. This is driving me nuts. Can't wait till Thursday. I'm at peace when I'm with you."

So apparently, I was going to have to pay for the mooring ball after all. When they were out in the ocean on a mooring ball, it was with a different marina than the one they were towed in on. Either Chad wasn't the best at communicating things, or I was easily confused. I believe it was a little of both.

I usually never brought my debit or credit cards to work, but for some reason I had them on me that day. I paid the fee, and it ended up being $94.60 (RED FLAG). I was going to be so happy when he finally was able to go to the bank. I knew he was frustrated because I was starting to get frustrated, too. I started questioning and wondering to myself if he would ever pay me back.

Later that evening I needed to buy our tickets to Epcot for when one of my daughters, her husband, and my grandson were going because I told her I would join them. Well now that Chad was in the picture, I wanted him to join us too. He kept mentioning Universal Studios and seeing Optimus prime, so I decided to buy our tickets to Epcot, Universal, and Islands of Adventure. If I was going to Universal, then I wanted to see Harry Potter World at Islands of Adventure too. I also had to get us a place to stay while we were in Orlando. Altogether the tickets and hotel equaled $843.18. I was getting excited about it all and it was just a couple weeks away. I like a good amusement park just as much as the next person. While I was buying the Epcot and Universal tickets, I decided to buy our plane tickets to my parents' house in Seattle for in July over my dad's eightieth birthday. That was just before my youngest daughter's wedding in Alabama, so I was cutting it close, but I didn't want to miss out on celebrating my dad. The longer you wait, the more expensive the tickets are, so I needed to go ahead and purchase them. Now that we were a couple, we would do everything together. I was excited for my parents and family to meet Chad. The plane tickets ended up being about $667.20 each.

While booking plane tickets to Seattle, I thought it would be nice to fly down to Key West and spend some time with Chad in Marathon on the boat in June. I had a few days off in a row and that would be a perfect time to check out the area while at the same time enjoying some time off in the Keys. The tickets were very reasonable and a lot easier than driving, so I went ahead and purchased a round trip ticket for $202.40.

The next time we were able to talk, it seemed like we only talked about Universal Studios/Islands of Adventure and Disney World. We both were excited, like a couple of kids. It's been a long time since either one of us had been there. So much had changed in the many years either of us had been, so it would be like visiting a brand new park all over again. After doing some research and looking at what was new at each park, we had an idea of what we both wanted to do.

After we hung up Chad texted and said, "Jerry just asked me when I was going home to Alabama. Lol. I told him that's your home, I visit. Lol. He thought we were married because I keep saying when the wife gets here, or I have to get my phone just in case the wife calls. Lol."

I told him that was cute of Jerry. He's such a good person and doesn't know when people are joking or not. I also enjoyed it when Chad would call me his wife, even if he was joking. It made me feel like our future was solid.

Chapter 14

(Mother's Day)

It was May 5th, and Chad was driving my truck up from Marathon while I worked. When he made it to the apartment, Julia was there, so they decided to go to lunch together. She took him to our favorite pizza place, called Satchel's Pizza. She told me later that he was a gentleman and paid for their lunch. They seemed to get along great. Julia said when he got there, he was making sure my truck was all clean and shiny and even asked her if she thought I'd be okay with it. That made me feel good. I take good care of my things and if I let someone borrow anything of mine, I expect the same from them. Boyfriend or not.

Chad stayed with me and Julia that night. The next morning, we were on our way back to Alabama for Mother's Day weekend. This time he would get to meet my youngest daughter.

While on the road, I was wondering if my Bluetooth was hooked up because it was playing all the songs I liked, so I asked Chad if that was my music playing.

He said, "No hun, I made a playlist of all our favorite songs together. We seem to like similar stuff."

I thought that was the sweetest thing ever, to take the time to make a playlist of our songs. I was impressed. We turned it up and we sang like we were in the band. Sometimes road trips were so much fun like that.

Chad was paying for the gas until we crossed into Georgia. He said his card wouldn't work since it was out of state (RED FLAG). He said that the name change has messed everything up. I remembered I had my card stop when I was in a different state before too, so I understood how that could happen. But once again, I had to pay the rest of the way (RED FLAG). I didn't want to ruin this trip to Alabama, so I refrained from bringing money up.

As soon as we got to my house later that evening, we started where we left off with the laundry. Chad had also brought up a few things he wanted to store at my house since we would be living on the boat. He was making a little more room for my stuff since the boat was small enough already. One item was a portable air conditioning unit that I thought we might could have used on the boat and another item was a tall fan which was something else that would have been useful. I didn't question anything, I just made room for everything. There was also a boat cover, a bin full of used boat stuff, and more clothes.

I had plans to have pedicures with my two daughters the next day for Mother's Day, then on Sunday we were driving to my youngest daughter's house in South Alabama for a dinner she was making for us and her future in-laws.

Before the pedicure, I had two girlfriends that wanted to come over and meet Chad. Krissy and Amelia showed up around lunch time. I was not planning on fixing anything, but Chad offered to whip up some lunch for them. In no time he had a couple different dishes for us to try. It was very impressive. Krissy even mentioned that I needed to take notes from him, to be a better hostess. It was all in fun. I was telling them the story of us at Buc-ee's while we were out on the porch, and when we went inside where Chad was, and he started telling them the same story. I didn't have the heart to tell him I had already shared that with them. It was cute. We all had a good visit and as they were leaving, Krissy said that he was a keeper and to not mess it up.

It was time for my pedicure with my daughters. Chad stayed at my house to relax some. The girls let me know they were a bit concerned for me moving so fast with Chad. I understood and was promising them that I was happy.

Later that day while Chad and I were running errands, I wanted him to meet some of my friends at the hospital I worked at, so we made a stop. One of the girls was questioning Chad about everything. Chad got a little defensive at times being questioned by four people in a little room (RED FLAG). It probably felt like an interrogation to him. I figured he was just nervous but trying not to show it. In general, I thought it went well. It was important to me that my friends could meet Chad in person.

That night Chad and I relaxed on my couch while watching some tv. I was hoping that he could handle all the upcoming events I had planned. I was usually not that busy, but with meeting my one daughter and her family in Orlando, my other daughter's wedding, and my dad's eightieth birthday, it was a lot, even for me. I wouldn't have blamed him if he wanted to opt out on a few things. I probably would have.

The next morning, I woke up and noticed Chad was not in the room. I didn't think anything about it since he usually wakes up early. I dozed back off for a minute when Chad came into the room with a tray of breakfast which included juice, coffee, eggs, toast, strawberries, and roses. It was wonderful. He told me Happy Mother's Day and left me with breakfast in bed. I couldn't remember the last time anyone brought me breakfast in bed, if at all. I could totally get used to all of that. He definitely made me feel special.

I told him how much I appreciated it and he answered with how much he appreciated me and that was the least he could do. He added that when we finally got settled on the boat, we would take ourselves on a nice long trip somewhere. I liked the sound of that.

After breakfast, we packed up and took off to South Alabama for Chad to meet my youngest daughter and her fiancé. It was a three to four hour drive, depending on traffic, and if Chad was driving. I decided that I was going to be doing the driving.

My daughter was in the kitchen cooking when we showed up. I introduced them and we sat around making small talk. Everything seemed to go well, and I was hoping she would be okay with him coming to her wedding in July. Overall, I thought it was a nice visit, with no major setbacks. We slept on an air mattress she set up for us and we left the next morning to get back to Gainesville.

I was feeling much better about Chad meeting all of my kids, my grandson, and seeing where I lived and how I lived. It was extremely important to me for him to know my kids and for my kids to know him. I was ready for a new life with a new partner, and I wanted Chad and my daughters to not only know each other, but to get along and be comfortable around one another.

After what I felt like a very successful and fun little weekend with Chad and my daughters, it was time for me to get back to work and for Chad to get back to the boat. I filled up the gas tank and gave Chad another one hundred dollars to get down to Marathon Key (RED FLAG). I hoped that this was going to be the last time helping him out.

Chapter 15

(Apartment Building)

On May 10th, while I was at work, I was thinking about how happy I was with where my life was at, but I also needed to talk to Chad about his bank issue. I texted Chad telling him how much I loved him and that there was no one else I'd rather be with, and I thought we made a great pair.

He answered, "I love you too Niki Rae. Yes, we are, and we will be great together. I know this. I'm sad already sitting here with Jerry."

In my next text I was determined to ask about the money, so it went like this, "When you go to your bank, would you be able to transfer me the money I put on my credit card for all the marina stuff? I don't have enough in savings to cover that plus the Disney/airline tickets, etc. I really hate asking and wish I didn't have to, but I wasn't expecting the marina fees, they ended up being $1,800.00. Then half of the Disney/Universal and Seattle tickets came to $1,000.00. I know it's a lot, and we definitely could use a mini vacation after the first half of the year. And you are the one who wanted to go to universal. Maybe not Epcot or Seattle, but you did agree. We will have fun though. I really hate asking anyone for any help, but the past few months I've been paying for three rents and only living in one. So, it's been stressing me out. I know you've put out a bunch on the boat, and I hated to even say anything, but now I have to. You have no idea how hard it is for me to ask for help. I'll work overtime, sell shit, whatever I have to do before I ask for help. But then I'm really not asking for help, I'm just asking for half of our vacation and marina expenses, right? I can send you the receipts for everything if you want me to."

His reply was, "Headed to the bank tomorrow. I'll call you tonight."

I didn't hear from him that evening, so I called him after my shift at work was over, no answer (RED FLAG). I was drained from work and fell asleep.

The next morning Chad text saying, "Just woke up hun. I slept on my phone and didn't hear it. Good morning sweetheart."

I told him good morning, but I had to get back to work and that I would talk to him later.

He said, "I woke up and Jerry was missing. Left me a note about how he met Cubans and has been here for ten years. Lol. He will be back."

A little later he texted, "He's back. Scrubbing the freeboard now as I clean up the engine room and get motors started. We are going to Key West tomorrow morning. My bank guy has appointments today, so I scheduled mine for in the morning. Jerry wants to go tomorrow too when the wind dies down so he can get to his boat. I'm going to drop him off and go to the bank. Besides that, I'm busting my ass on the boat today. I hope you're having a great day sweetheart. I miss you already. Feels like I'm missing something."

I told him I was missing him, too, and I couldn't wait until next week when we were going to Disney.

I was busy at work the next morning when he texted, "Hi hun."

I replied, "Hi there, how's your day so far?"

"It's going. Half of the boat is cleaned up. Had to have a talk with Jerry about keeping clean and keeping the boat clean. I didn't like the mess I came back to. Frustrating. Just took him to the store so he can get bait and ice. Can't wait to wake up next to you again. Can't wait to cook for you again."

"I can't wait either," I said.

"I have an appointment for the truck on Thursday as well to go into the shop and get fluids done and a checkout all over," Chad replied. I thought that was fine of him.

I was busy at work and not able to look at my phone for a few hours. When I was able to look at my phone, I saw texts from Chad, saying that he noticed I accidentally dialed him, then hung up. He texted multiple times asking if I was okay. Then he was saying I was making him nervous. When I finally was able to respond, I let him know that I was busy with a patient and wasn't able to look at my phone. He was so relieved, thinking something happened to me. I told him that that was how I felt when I didn't hear from him for hours at a time. It was not a good feeling.

Chad sent me a picture of a table with driftwood underneath, telling me if we decide to stay in Alabama, we could make those as a side gig. He had been mentioning living in Alabama more frequently, but I really wanted to live in Florida on a boat. I knew he was just talking, so I let him talk.

While we were talking on the phone, I mentioned I downloaded the money transfer app he talked about previously so he could transfer me the money I was waiting for. He said as soon as the bank clears that he would transfer me five grand. For some reason It was taking longer than it should have (RED FLAG).

The next day I tried calling with no answer. I wanted another update on how the bank's progress was going. Later Chad texted, "Hi hun. Doing errands in Key West. I'll call tonight. Truck is going up in the air on the lift in half an hour. Injectors are dirty. O2 sensor may be going. Checking everything today. I'll call tonight sweetheart. I hope you're having a wonderful day today. I love you. Dropped Jerry off so he can go work at Mustafa's and check on his boat."

I thought it was cordial of him to get my truck serviced. With all the salty air, it was probably a good idea. Plus, with both of us using it, it's getting more miles on it. It was probably about time if not overdue for one.

Every once in a while, I would look on the tracker to see where he was. He was usually where he said, but occasionally he was at an apartment building. Chad said the apartment belonged to a fishing buddy of his (RED FLAG). He would sometimes have dinner with his buddy and his wife and kids. I had no reason to doubt him. Relationships are all based on trust. And I trusted him.

That afternoon and evening I was texting him with no response. I was asking if everything was okay and that I was getting worried and stressing out. It was getting late and my last text to him was telling him that I was going to take a Xanax to sleep, because I couldn't take not hearing from him for hours at a time, especially when he had my truck. I was trying to think positive thoughts while falling asleep.

The next morning Chad texted, "Jerry just cried to me about his mom. Apparently today is the day she died. The anniversary. That's why he is acting weird. Sometimes I feel like I'm playing big brother to a handicap child."

I thought it was very sweet of him to be there for a friend, and I told him that Jerry needed him, and it was a good thing he was there to listen. He said Jerry was finally sleeping, that he cried for four hours. I said sometimes you just need a good cry.

Chad then said, "How's your day going sweetheart? Feeling better? I can't wait to breath you in. I miss your scent."

I said, "I miss you too. And I was wondering if you could look to see if my little black dress is on the boat and if you could bring it to me next week?"

"Yes dear. I'll hunt for it. And if it's found I'll put it right in the truck. It's probably right in the V birth. And if it's not there it is probably in the back seat of Cookies car. Lol. That was a joke hun," he replied.

"Oh my! You are not going to let me forget about that are you?"

He texted while laughing, "Never. All I know is the first day we met, your friend is handing you a dress you left in the backseat of some car. I don't know the background. I just got there. I mean, lol."

I told him it was a bathing suit not a dress. And for someone who forgets a lot, he definitely wasn't forgetting about that (RED FLAG). He said because that one was a brick. We laughed about that. I added that we both have had bricks thrown at us.

Chad said, "I've never strayed from you. You have no worries about me sweetheart. Since we've met, I've been all about you. No one else. Didn't have time or the want. I've never gone on dates with anyone or betrayed you in any way. Seriously hun. I'm not going anywhere. Just letting you know you don't have to worry about me in any way. So don't think bad things about me."

"I'm not thinking bad things," I replied, wondering where that came from.

The next day I said my "good morning" and asked how he was.

"Everything's going ok. Hung out with my buddy last night. Needed time away from Jerry. Had a BBQ. Smoked a bowl and fell asleep. I don't normally smoke weed. Makes me tired," he replied.

I told him I was sorry he was in a funk, and that I wasn't doing the greatest either. We exchanged a few more messages and then I didn't hear from him the rest of the day. At first, I wasn't too worried, life happens. But after not getting a quick text about if something was wrong, anxiety started setting in. I texted him multiple times to let him know I was getting worried. Eventually my worry was high enough I texted asking if there was something I needed to know. He was making my stomach turn. I looked on the tracker and he was at that apartment building again. That was where he said he was, but for two nights? (RED FLAG). He needed to be on the boat fixing it up for us. I was starting to get upset with him when I heard a knock at my door.

My daughter and her family showed up that evening of May 15th to stay with me before they headed to Orlando. They showed up at the perfect time. They would help me not to think about Chad. It was their Disney vacation time, and Chad and I planned on joining them in a few days at Epcot. The plan was for Chad to drive my truck back up to me in two days, then we would head to Orlando for two nights. Chad knew this, so not hearing from him was very stressful.

After a slightly restless night, I took my daughter and her family to the Sweetwater Wetlands where I would walk and jog quite often. It was my happy place, very peaceful with all kinds of wildlife. Every day there were alligators and birds hanging out, but once in a while deer, turtles, and snakes would come out, too. The scenery was beautiful, and we all enjoyed it that morning. Once it started getting hot my daughter decided it was time for lunch and then off to Orlando for them.

I was glad one of my daughters finally came to see where I was living and working at. It was already May and I had been in Gainesville since January. They were the first visitors I've had. Julia was there so they were able to meet her, too.

I messaged Chad a few times with no response. As hard as it was, I tried not to let it get to me. I had two more days of work, then Orlando. It was coming up fast and I really couldn't believe how Chad could just ignore me and not respond. He had my truck, and he was supposed to be driving it up in two days. I had made all these plans. I wasn't sure what I would do if he didn't show up as planned. I was guessing I would have to fly down there to get my truck. Is he seeing someone, is that why he is not responding? Did something happen? Is he hurt? Did he get in an accident? Is that it? Am I ever going to hear from him again? I couldn't shut my brain off. When I looked on the tracker, he was all over Key West. That helped me know at least he was up and moving around. Unless someone else had his phone. I needed something to do to keep from thinking of all the bad thoughts. Aggravated, I decided to pack for Orlando. Packing definitely helped me become less irritable and more excited for the trip.

The next day I texted Chad, asking about his day.

He finally replied, "Blah. Selling the bike today."

"I'm sorry you feel blah...you better not be that way after you get up here or I'll have to kick your ass!" I said, and added, "Anyways, I don't mean to add to your blah day, and I hate to ask, but are you able to send that money from the tickets/marina through cash app? My credit cards are due, and I don't have enough to pay them off and I hate paying interest. I haven't had a balance in years. I would so, so much appreciate it. It stresses me out to ask, I wish I didn't have to."

He said, "As soon as this paperwork is done, then yes. That's all I'm waiting for to start my way up there."

"I think you also need a good night's sleep tonight. Jerry seems to be wearing you out!"

"That's exactly what I need," he replied.

I was so glad he was finally responding. A big weight was lifting. I was also able to ask for the money back, which was super hard for me to do. I had been waiting so long that it was starting to infuriate me. I was letting him use my truck while I was paying for everything. I didn't mind helping at all, especially when I'm with someone, but it goes both ways. Plus, he said he didn't touch his pension and had rental money coming in. What was the hold up? I didn't understand.

It was now the day before Chad needed to drive up and I was hoping he was ready. I asked him if everything was okay. He said yes and he was waiting on Jerry. I asked him if Jerry was staying on the boat while he was with me. He said yes, that was the plan.

"Did you sell your bike?" I asked.

"Not yet, Showing it again in ten minutes. I have a bunch of showings tonight."

I started thinking about keeping my truck with me after he drove it back up. It would be three to four weeks before I was in the Keys again. I felt like that was the only real thing I had of mine from my home. Sharing an apartment with a great new friend and sleeping on an air mattress was nice, but I missed having something that was really "mine". I said to Chad, "I think I'm going to keep my truck so you might not want to sale your bike just yet. I don't think I can do without it for six weeks. I have girlfriends I need to go visit before I'm done here. I need to be able to get away when I want to. To go for a ride with my music turned up. I would miss that."

"That's fine. Getting rid of bike anyway. I never asked for the truck," Chad replied.

"I know you didn't. I wasn't saying anything about you having it. I was just saying I'm going to need it since I will be here six more weeks and I hate relying on someone else. It's been fine so far because it's been short intervals."

He answered back, "I'm ready to move to Alabama and start a fish and reptile tank business. Lol."

He called me later and he told me he took his bike to a pawn shop and got some money to pay for gas to make it back up to me, because the bank was taking too long. He said it was a friend of his who works there and that he would hold his bike until he got back. That way he would have some money with him.

We also talked about fish tanks, and he told me how he had learned all about them and was good at it. Chad said it would be a great side job and we could make a lot of money in it. I listened but I was not interested. I wanted to live in Florida where it was sunny and warm year round. I believed he was in a down mood with everything and just brainstorming ideas. I didn't think too much about it. It was time for both of us to get some rest, I had to work the next day and he was going to be driving eight hours (well ten for him) to be with me. We said our good nights and I love you's and hung up.

I couldn't stop thinking and wondering what he was thinking about. It seemed like he was changing his mind about us living on the boat at the marina in

Marathon. When we visited, I thought it was really a nice place and I could see myself living there. I could work at the local hospital and maybe even volunteer or work at the local aquarium they had there. I was pulling for Marathon, and he was pulling for Alabama. We would have to talk more in person of our plans and what we wanted, because right now it didn't seem to be lining up with what the other one wanted.

The next morning, he showed me a picture of the gas tank being eight miles to empty. I told him he was living on the edge, and that picture about gave me a heart attack. He said he was getting all the bad fuel out and getting ready to put fresh new fuel in, to try to make the truck happy for its drive up to me. He also told me to relax and stop stressing, that everything was going to be okay.

I said, "You promise?"

He said, "Yes dear."

I sure hoped so. It seemed like lately we've been running into obstacles that were making us unsure of our plans. I told him I had a hard time not worrying because I've always been an organized and planned-out person and knew my future. But right then I was all out of sorts because my life was all over the place. I really just needed a hug from him and for him to tell me it would be alright.

The next text Chad sent was all about this dinosaur he picked up to give to my grandson. He said it was a big one and it was sitting in the passenger seat, and he couldn't wait to give it to him. Chad was so excited about it and sent me lots of pictures and texts about his new riding buddy.

I was thinking how thoughtful of him to buy my grandson a toy, he would love that.

He told me that the tail was sticking out of a trash can at a yard sale, but it looked to be in perfect condition, so he had to check it out. When he went to inspect it to make sure nothing was broken, nothing was wrong with it! Chad said he knew he had to get it right then. He did not stop talking about that dinosaur for a while.

I giggled to myself thinking how cute it was that he was that excited about a dinosaur. It didn't bother me that he got it out of a trash can. I trusted him. I go to yard sales all the time and come across great finds. I've also been dumpster diving looking for wood pieces that I could use for crafts, so I had nothing to say about that. I knew my grandson was going to like it, too.

Chapter 16

(Panic Attack)

May 18th, Chad finally made it to Gainesville. It was late and I was already in bed, but I couldn't sleep while waiting on him. We had a nice quiet reunion and we both fell asleep tangled up in each other's arms.

The next morning, we were up and packing the truck up for our trip to Orlando. While sitting on the tailgate, I brought it up to Chad again that I wanted to keep my truck and we needed to figure out how to get him back to Key West after our Orlando trip. He was instantly upset and started saying that he wasn't expecting this, and he had some jobs lined up for when he got back (RED FLAG). He said he was going to have to make some phone calls. Chad pulled out a cigarette looking very stressed and started pacing back and forth. That was the first time I had seen him that unsettled. I already told him in a text a few days prior that I was going to keep my truck, and I had also told him he might not want to sell his bike. I remember him acknowledging my text, so I was confused as to why he reacted like that. It was like that was the first time he was hearing about it.

Then I asked, "Are you broke?"

He replied, "No, I'm not broke, I'm still waiting on the bank to clear me, and I'm not used to not being able to get to my accounts. I've been looking into a job at the fish store, and they want me to take over as the manager and I have an appointment to see an officer at the correction facility in Marathon to work as a guard there also. I just have a lot going on and a lot on my mind. And now I need to figure out what to do since I won't have a vehicle to get around on."

I went back inside the apartment to get the cooler feeling kind of bad. Julia was up and I told her what Chad just told me and how he seemed on edge. She asked me, "Why do you need your truck? I have an extra car here, we can make it work, you don't need your truck."

I was even more confused now and told her, "Well, that's the only thing that's mine here and I just like having it. But no, you're right, I don't 'need' it."

I had already booked a flight to Key West for in June, so I could always drive Red back up then if I needed to. That would be four weeks away. Could I manage for four weeks without my truck? A month sounded like a long time. Yet I really didn't need it, like Julia said; it's just a truck. However, she didn't know how attached I was to that truck. I had just bought it the summer before, and I had made multiple trips home and to Key West in it, plus I had just paid it off on May 13th. That was a huge deal to me. I worked hard for that truck, I even named it Red. I had never owned anything that cost that much before in my life. The thought of letting it go for an extra four weeks was making me a little anxious. Although, seeing how out of sorts and slightly depressed Chad was acting, I thought maybe I should just let him use it. I didn't want him acting like that the whole time we were in Orlando, stressing about getting back home to Key

West. I wanted us to have a good time, not for it to be ruined by me not letting him use my truck. I decided that Julia was right, it wouldn't hurt me to let him take my truck after all (RED FLAG).

I went back outside to tell Chad not to worry, that he could use my truck. I let him know I could borrow Julia's second car when I needed to. He was a little confused at first, but then instantly he started to be himself again.

When the truck was all packed and ready to go, we were on our way to Orlando. It was a nice ride. We talked about his family and how he had an uncle (Chad's mom's brother) that lived in Gainesville that he hadn't seen in years. In fact, the last time he saw him was when his mom died at least twenty-five years ago. His Uncle told Chad that Chad was the reason she died. After his own uncle blamed him for the death of his mom, Chad walked away and hadn't seen him since. After letting go of some of the hard feelings he developed, Chad was thinking about possibly going to see his uncle when we got back from Orlando. I told him that I supported him, and I would be there by his side if that's what he wanted to do. He told me he was a lucky man to be with someone like me.

Another conversation we had was talking about how Chad wanted to live in Alabama for a little bit. Chad mentioned that since he cut everyone off and stopped helping people financially, no one wanted to be his friend anymore. He felt like things were changing, and not in a good way. The feeling of needing to get away was getting stronger for him. The best thing he could think of was starting fresh, somewhere new, like Alabama. He said we wouldn't stay in Alabama forever, just to refocus and rejuvenate our ideas and plans.

For some reason I did not want him living in Alabama with me (RED FLAG). I'm not sure if it was that I didn't want him moving into my house with me, or something else. I really couldn't put my finger on it, but I felt unsettled by the thought of him staying in Alabama. My dream was to live near the water in Florida, or on a boat and get a place that we could rent out. I liked the idea of me doing odd jobs and working part time at a hospital. I wanted excitement and adventure. I wanted a place the kids and my friends and family would love to come visit, a place that had no history with either one of us, somewhere new. We really didn't come to an agreement on that subject, so that was a disappointment, but we also didn't argue about it, either, which was favorable.

Our deep conversations died when we arrived in Orlando. We checked in and invited my daughter, her husband, and my grandson over to hang out at our pool before we all went out to dinner. Chad could not wait to give my grandson the dinosaur. Chad had the dinosaur sitting in the pool when they arrived. My grandson remembered Chad and he was excited about the dinosaur. Chad was like a kid playing with a kid. My son-in-law even mentioned how Chad needed a rent-a-kid fix. Chad had always wanted kids but never had any, so I agreed with my son-in-law on the renting a kid idea. He was so attentive to my grandson; I think he would have made a great dad.

Chad and I found a Chuck-E-Cheese nearby and thought that would be a great place for my grandson. Plus, who doesn't like pizza and beer? My son-in-law disagreed and wanted to go somewhere where they had steak. It took a while for all of us to agree on something, but we ended up at a Japanese restaurant. The wait was a little long, but the food was good. There wasn't much for a three year old to do, though. He was getting a little restless by the time we all finished eating. Chad and my son-in-law paid our bills and since it was getting late it was time for everyone to get some rest before Epcot the next day.

That evening we had a wonderful time in our hotel relaxing before our mini Disney vacation. I was just as excited as Chad was. It was like when you arrive in Orlando you turn into a kid, no matter what your age is. It's just magical like that. It's been quite some time since I've been to one of the Disney parks. I was also looking forward to spending time with my daughter and her family, and to watch Chad when he finally sees Optimus Prime.

The next morning Chad drove us and paid for our parking to get in. I was glad he finally had some money. I didn't really care if he pawned his bike or not, as long as he was able to pay finally. He said he would get the bike back when he returned to Key West.

We found my daughter and her family in the park, and they were already waiting in line to see one of the characters. While waiting with them, Chad left for a minute and came back with a glass of wine for me and an ice cream for himself and my grandson. I was thinking that this was the way it was supposed to be. I liked it, and it made me love him a little bit more. He helped out with keeping an eye on my grandson since he was only three. We all had a good time, eating new foods and getting our pictures made with Mickey Mouse. Chad joined in on everything without any resistance.

Later in the evening Chad and I were wearing paper hats we accumulated earlier in the day, and all of a sudden here comes a Florida downpour. We ran for cover, but not before we got soaked, which made our hats cling to our heads. We looked so silly and laughed so hard about that. The rain did not stop us from having a good time, and we waited it out then hopped on another ride.

We all said our goodbyes at the end of such a fun and magical day, then went to our hotels. It was time for Chad and I to get ready for the next day at Universal Studios and Islands of Adventure, followed by a two hour drive back to Gainesville. We made the most of our evening and being alone.

Chad paid for parking the next morning and once again, I was feeling a little relief. It's been a long time coming for Chad to be paying for anything.

190

As soon as we entered the gate to Universal Studios, we had to beeline our way to Optimus Prime. We could go and do whatever after that Chad said, but in order for him to die happy he absolutely had to meet Optimus Prime. Luckily there was no waiting. If you wanted to meet Optimus Prime, you had to ride the ride first. When the ride was over, I agreed that it was pretty fun. Chad was already having the time of his life. We waited in line for him to get a picture with Optimus Prime, his favorite Transformer. You would have thought he was ten years old and seeing his idol for the first time ever. He could now die in peace he said. I was happy to see him so happy.

The day was a blast. We rode the best roller coaster I had ever been on at Islands of Adventure called VelociCoaster. You had to take everything off, including watches and other jewelry, and put them in a locker for safekeeping, then go through a scanner before getting on the ride. It was thrilling. If the line wasn't so long, and if Chad's stomach wasn't a little queasy, we would have ridden it again. Then there was Harry Potter World, it was better than I had imagined it to be. It was fun watching the kids with their magical wands opening and closing things. The Harry Potter train ride from Universal to Islands of Adventure was just like in the movie too. Disney is on point!

By then it was lunchtime and we needed to eat something other than the snacks I brought in my backpack. This time I had to pay, since his money had ran out. He only received so much money for the scooter and after paying for gas, food and parking, his pockets were empty (RED FLAG). That was definitely disappointing and once again I was footing the bill. I bought us some hoagie sandwiches, which were so big, we each saved half for later. I was happy with that deal.

We decided to go ahead and head out since we saw everything we wanted to see, plus some. It was a great two days. When we made it to the parking lot, neither one of us remembered where we parked. We spent a while looking for Red with no luck, until we realized we were on the wrong level. We both did not remember going down an escalator that morning. It made for a good laugh. We then drove back to the apartment I was staying at and crashed as soon as we hit the bed.

The next morning Chad was talking about going to see his uncle. He found his address and was getting up the nerve to take a drive to go see him. Chad was so nervous and was even more frazzled when he found out his uncle lived only about twenty minutes from the apartment. A few minutes later we were off to see his uncle. I rode along for support and was hoping his uncle would be there, since we were showing up unannounced.

As we turned the corner, we could see his uncle's house and we spotted him outside pressure washing his driveway. Chad told me to stay in the truck for a minute. I watched as Chad walked up to his uncle, who seemed curious, then suspicious. They said a few words, then there was a hug. I was so relieved it turned out positive. Chad motioned me to come on out. We were introduced and he immediately took us in his house for a drink and conversation. It was an older house, and there were pictures and collectibles all over from Chad's childhood. I listened to stories of them growing up and about Chad's mom. Chad's uncle's wife came home, and we listened as they reminisced about old times. I sat next to Chad as he was looking through an old family album that had his mom in it. I looked up at him to see that he was about to cry. I held his hand to let him know that I was with him. He was happy he could see pictures of his mom again. It was great to see him reconnect with his uncle and aunt, and to see pictures of him as a child. It was a very surreal moment.

I couldn't imagine being alone in this world without family. I was glad he decided to see his uncle, and that it turned out to be a good decision. Everyone needed some family in their lives, even if you are not in the same city. All of my family is out West (minus my girls), but they are always there for me with open arms if I come visit, and we talk on a regular basis. I am very lucky.

We left after a few hours. I mentioned that it was a good time, and I'm glad he was able to reconnect after all this time. Chad had mixed emotions about his uncle. He wasn't sure if he wanted to see him again or not. I listened to all his childhood stories that involved his uncle that he wanted to tell. I was glad I was able to be there for him.

The next day I had to work, and Chad stayed at the apartment relaxing. He had said he had a major headache, and he could hardly move. He stayed on the bed resting the whole day. I told him that maybe he needed to stay a few more days then, until he feels better. He seemed surprised when I meantioned that, but he immediately said it could be a possibility if he made some phone calls. He said he'd have to do some laundry and cook for me and Julia one night.

On my day off I took Chad to the sweet water wetlands to walk around and see the alligators. It was a nice sunny day as usual, and we were the only ones on this particular trail. Chad pulled out a joint he brought from Key West and started to smoke it. He said he didn't smoke to get high. A while back he got a medical card and he only used weed for when he was in pain. Usually he used a pen, but this time he chose to get a joint. He asked if I wanted a hit. I work in the medical field so that is something I never do, but at that moment I decided why not. It only took one hit for me to be feeling pretty free. I was fine for a moment, then all of a sudden, I started having these weird feelings about Chad. My breathing started getting faster and shallow, my heart rate went up, I couldn't speak, and I was in a panic mode. I couldn't get my breathing under control and even felt a little nauseous, and even thought I might pass out. It felt like I was on the verge of having a panic attack, if I wasn't already in the middle of one. I had never had one before, so I wasn't sure what was going on, but I felt so out of control and scared.

Chad looked at me and said, "Are you alright? You are awfully quiet and pale."

With a panicked look on my face, and trying to keep it together, I was finally able to speak and said, "Not really..." I looked up at him and all these racing thoughts came out of my mouth. "Are you going to steal my truck? Are you going to take me out on your boat and chop me up in little pieces and then dump me in the ocean? Are you going to take me for everything I have?" (RED FLAG)

Chad looked shocked and then said seriously, "Holy Crap! Where is this coming from? No more weed for you. And no, I'm not going to do anything to you, and I never asked for your truck anyways."

He grabbed me and we just hugged, while my breathing was still fast. He told me everything was going to be okay and to not worry. After taking some deep breaths, I felt a little better, and a whole lot better after the high went away. I decided I was never doing that again. Not being in control of my own thoughts and emotions was scary and not fun. I hated that feeling. I wasn't even sure why my thoughts went in that direction (RED FLAG), but they did.

We made it back to the apartment and decided to take it easy the rest of the day. The next day, Julia and I were off to work and rode together in her car. There was no sense in taking two vehicles when we worked the same hours in the same department. Later that day Chad let me know he took my truck to go see his uncle again. He said he was feeling a little better, but only fifty-fifty. I wasn't sure how I felt about him taking Red to go do whatever he wanted without asking or telling me first. It was something that I was going to have to get used to once we started living together, so I didn't say anything (RED FLAG). Chad said he would have dinner ready for Julia and me when we got home. I told him he didn't have to do that, but he said it was relaxing for him and he loved to cook. I was wondering what on earth would he be cooking for us; we didn't have much in the apartment.

When Julia and I walked in after work, Chad had a whole meal and a salad sitting on the table for us, looking very inviting. Even the presentation was beautifully laid out. It was like we had our own chef. Chad used only what we had in the apartment, but it looked wonderful. I would never have figured out how to make a meal out of what little we had. Not only did it look good, but it also tasted good. Needless to say, both Julia and I were impressed.

Chad stayed for a couple more days. I had given Chad one hundred dollars to get back to Marathon on a few days prior when I thought he was leaving. He kept going back and forth to the gas station for whatever reason, and I told him that he better make the one hundred dollars last until he gets to Marathon. It pretty much felt like I was treating him like one of my kids; giving him an allowance, and when it ran out it ran out. Chad mentioned staying with me a few more days, but I told him no. I had to work over the weekend, which equaled working four days in a row. It was time for him to get back to the boat and start fixing it up. I felt like he had enough time off and should be all rested up. I told him it would make me mad if I was working while he was running around doing whatever. I told him that he needed to get down to the boat and start working on it. I had a plane ticket to fly down there in June to hang out for a few days and I wanted the boat somewhat cleaned up by then. It was quite the mess last time I seen it. He didn't seem thrilled with me saying no, but he agreed to leave.

That evening we loaded up a few things of mine that I wanted to leave on the boat, my cooler filled with drinks, a lunch, and snacks, all ready for an eight hour drive. I also wanted Chad to take my bicycle with him since I was going to be there in a few weeks, and it would be nice if we took some bike rides together. Chad got excited about that, and in order for the bike to fit in the truck bed with the top covering it, we had to take the front tire off of it. After everything was loaded, we turned in for a good night's sleep. It was time for Chad to leave and go back to work on the boat. Most importantly, it was time for him to go to the bank and get ahold of his money.

The next morning on May 28th, I went to work while Chad took my truck, bicycle, and personal items with him to Marathon.

Chapter 17

(Lies)

It was a busy day at work so I wasn't able to chat with Chad as much as I would have liked while he was on his way to Marathon. We talked a few times, but that was it. He tried calling me in the middle of the day, but I was unable to answer. He let me know when he made it to Key West. When I was able to, I texted him telling him that I was glad he made it, and I was sorry I couldn't answer his call.

After I got to the apartment that night, I tried calling Chad but there was no answer. I decided to look on the tracker to see where he was. He was in Key West, not Marathon, at the apartment building that he was at often (RED FLAG). That was the same apartment building that he said a buddy of his lived at. I instantly felt uneasy and annoyed. Chad should be at the boat, but he drove past the marina in Marathon, where the boat was, and drove an hour further into Key West. He was putting more miles on my truck to go to some apartment building. I was so furious that I threw the phone down and went straight to bed.

The next morning after waking up I checked my phone right away. My phone had a notification that Chad had stopped sharing his location on the tracker (RED FLAG). The stopping time was just after I looked the night before at 7:12pm, when he was at the apartment building in Key West. My heart did a skip, and I knew at that moment that something wasn't right. Who was it that he was seeing there? My stomach was in knots. I really didn't know what to do besides take him off my location, too. Of course, he would see a notification like I did with his, but I didn't care.

Just under the notification that he stopped sharing his location, he had texted at 9:59pm saying, "Woke up for a minute. Noticed I missed your call. I fell asleep lol. I'm going back to sleep now. I'll call you in the morning. Good night sweetheart. I filled out the application for the sheriff's office. I love you. Sleep well."

Chad was making me furious and giving me a sick feeling. I didn't want him catching on that I knew he was in Key West at that apartment building, more so because he had my truck. If I called him out and made him mad, there was no telling what he would do. I texted him before I went to work, telling him good morning and that I hoped he had a good day. That was May 29th.

I didn't hear from him all day. That provoked my anger even more. I was at a loss about what to do. My gut was telling me that something really wasn't right (RED FLAG). Why would he take me off the tracker like that? Why go all the way into Key West when we are going to be living on a boat that was in Marathon? More importantly, what was he hiding?

I had a feeling and just knew that he wasn't going to pay for June's rent at the marina, and there was no way in hell I was going to pay for yet another month's rent. I had already paid for the past three months, plus other fees I wasn't expecting. June was just two days away and my credit card was the one on file for payment, with the bill due at the first of the month. Thank goodness I had already paid off the credit card I used, so the decision that night to cancel it and cut it up was easy. I felt better already.

Still no word from Chad. I went to bed praying about what I should do. I wasn't feeling all fuzzy anymore. Instead, I was feeling shaken up and very unsure of my future. At this point, I was wondering if I even made the right choice to live on a boat in the first place. I prayed to God for clarity, for guidance and the truth, or a sign to help me to know what to do. I felt like I messed up and was getting taken advantage of.

After a restless night and waking up early, it was now May 30th. No new texts or missed calls. I texted Chad telling him good morning and that I had hoped I would have heard from him by now. I also took a half of a Xanax to calm my nerves so I could be calm at work while I was trying to figure out what I should do.

He texted right back saying, "Good morning sweetheart. Just came back to shore to call you in the morning. We've been out fishing the banks. I love you sweetheart."

A little later I received another text: "Hello again sweetheart. Called a few times. I know you're busy. My buddy and I have been doing some fishing for the holiday weekend. We are going back out today for a bit. I love you. I hope your day goes smooth. I'll talk to you this afternoon."

It wasn't long and he text again saying, "I was just trying to get a call in before we headed offshore. All fueled up. Headed back out to the reef to fish some more. I love you. Have a wonderful day today."

I finally had a chance to text, "Sorry I missed your call, we are pretty busy here. Have fun. I picked up an extra day this week which will make five days total. So, I will be living at work this week."

After getting some free time, I was looking at my phone and saw a notification in an area I never look at. I clicked on it. It was someone who was not on my friends list but was messaging me through Facebook messenger in an odd way. So, I opened it up. The message was dated April 30th. If it had been there this whole time, it had been there a whole month, and I was just then seeing it. It read:

"Hi Niki Rae, this is for your info only. Please do not share this with Chad. I am reaching out to you because I have concerns for your safety and financial wellbeing. I am one of the apparently many recent female victims of Chad's manipulation. Can you confirm with me that this conversation won't be shared with Chad, for all our safety? If you would like, perhaps we could have a chat by phone or zoom? I don't do much on Facebook, and I don't know well enough how it works. I am hesitant to add you as a friend, or even if you would add me as a friend. I hope that sending a message like this allows you to still send a message back to me without us first having to be 'friends' first. Please don't give him any more money. He hasn't paid me back yet and I really needed the money. You seem way too wonderful to be taken for a ride by Chad." (HUGE RED FLAG).

My heart stopped and my stomach dropped to my feet! I instantly felt nauseated, my legs got weak, and I had to sit down. When I felt a little better and could think, despite what the messenger advised, I showed my friends at work and the first thing they said was, "You have to go get your truck!"

How did I miss this message? All of my unexpected gut feelings were telling me something wasn't right. I should have listened to them more carefully.

The first thing my friends and I decided to do was look up the name that Chad said he was changing it to. I never even thought to look it up earlier since we were deep in a relationship by then. One of my coworkers had a bachelor's degree in criminal justice, so she knew where to look. The first thing that popped up without research was that a masked man robbed a bank.... The other individual of interest in that robbery was Chad....

I was so glad I took half a Xanax that morning. It was more than I could deal with. I was very thankful for the friends I was working with. They all were patient with me and very supportive. The more we researched, the more we found. I wasn't sure how much information I could absorb after what I read.

The next thing we found was "United States V. Chad…", seaman recruit, U.S. Coastguard. He was separated from the Coast Guard with six months confinement and a bad conduct discharge while undergoing recruit training. It started when he was notified of his mother's death and was allowed to leave to attend the funeral. After his return, he began to exhibit symptoms of extreme stress. This manifested into depression, crying spells, confusion, loss of appetite and weight loss. He apparently even began to hallucinate about his mother, all leading to an unauthorized absence. He was also convicted of fraudulent enlistment, and false statement of the uniform code of military justice.

So, he was never a Ranger for twenty years, no pension, no money. How could I have been so fooled? It made me sick. My mind was in shock. It was so hard to concentrate and work in-between researching and finding new information about the man I loved and wanted to spend the rest of my life with.

We then found out that Chad had an active warrant out for his arrest, which explained why he was always driving so slowly. He was in jail a few times, he had a grand theft of $15,000.00 against him, removal from a property, a restraining order against him three years prior, and he was actively on probation. We also found out that he was in business with a lady for a year or two. That business went inactive one month before I met him, and he was not allowed to use the business to obtain any loans. The address of the business was the same address or area that he seemed to always be hanging out at. Chad said that that was where his fishing buddy lived and that was who he was hanging out with when he was at that location. It was also the last area he was at before he took me off his tracker on his phone.

When I was able to somewhat process all the information, I had lots of questions that I knew wouldn't be answered, at least not anytime soon. Was he seeing his old business partner? Why did she cut him off? If he was staying the night there, was it just a business building or were there apartments there, too?

Besides feeling sick to my stomach, my adrenaline was pumping. I felt so stupid! Everything I knew was a lie. What was this guy capable of? How am I going to get my truck? I couldn't shut my mind off. Disbelief and shock took over my whole body. My head was spinning. This was not happening to me.

When I gained my composure, I had to think. First thing was I needed to go get my truck. I had no idea what he was planning. The only day I had off that week was Wednesday, June 1st. It looked like I would be buying a one-way ticket to Key West. I had to make up a story and I had to pretend to still be the girlfriend that didn't know anything. I didn't want him doing anything crazy to my truck or to me.

My whole future had just changed in an instant. All from an anonymous tip on Facebook messenger that I was supposed to have read a month ago. But after praying all night, God made it visible to me. That was my sign. There were probably many other signs I ignored (which there were). God was patient with me, but He knew it was time. I'm not sure what I would have done if I had never read that message. It was time to start planning my excuse to go get my truck.

Julia had left a couple days earlier to drive one of her cars to Tennessee, so she wasn't at the apartment to help me. I was missing her something terrible. While I was brainstorming, I came up with her car breaking down on me. She did say it had some electrical issues at one time, so I was going to go with that.

I knew I was the worst liar, so I hoped I could sound convincing enough. I had called Julia earlier telling her everything and let her know that I was using her car as an excuse. She told me to go look in her bedroom for her safe to make sure it was still there. We had left Chad by himself a few times while we worked the week earlier. Thank goodness nothing was out of place.

Chad had said that him and his friend were going out fishing for the day, so my phone had been quiet all day. I was thankful for that. It was going to be awkward talking to him, knowing what I had just found out about him. Did he really think I would never find out?

That night I was on my phone looking up airline tickets and planning to go get my truck back.

It was May 31st, and I still hadn't heard from Chad. I texted him from work saying, "Good morning hun, I hope you have a great day, Love you!" Then I added, "It's crazy here at work. What are your plans today?"

He replied, "Good morning sweetheart. My day today is going to get parts for the boat. Driving now to go get parts. I hope your day goes smooth for you sweetheart."

He then sends me a picture of a hen with her two babies and says, "So I'm hanging out with this hot hen and two chicks she brought with her."

I just replied with, "aw."

Later in the afternoon I messaged him saying, "Hey hun, how's your day going? We've been busy here at work, so at least the time is going by fast. Only five weeks from today till I'm done! Woohoo!"

There was no reply from Chad. I was once again relieved.

I was able to purchase an airline ticket for the next morning, June 1st. I was so nervous about it all. Trying to keep up with the pretending was the hardest thing for me. I felt like I was walking on pins and needles. I was hoping my text messages or talking on the phone wouldn't show my tension and anxiousness.

Chad called in the evening, and we chatted as usual. I told him I was going to go so I could go to the store. He questioned me going to the store so late. I said I wanted some milk for my coffee for the next morning. Thankfully he accepted my lie. Then I waited almost an hour before I was going to tell him the car broke down. I was so nervous and shaking. I'd never done anything like that before, purposely lying because I knew something that I was not supposed to. I was not one for confrontation either, that was way out of my comfort zone. With my heart beating rapidly, I built up enough courage to call him. It went straight to voicemail, and I was relieved. I could then just text him and go from there.

This is what I said: "I tried calling, it went to voicemail, not a good night! Julia's car won't start, and a neighbor said it was probably the starter. I've been on the phone with Julia, and she said she's had electrical issues before and that she would come back early to take it to a shop. She mentioned for me to get my truck since we will need a vehicle. So, I looked up tickets and was able to get one to come down there tomorrow! I'll be there at 11am in Key West. I'll have to drive straight back since I work Thursday and Friday. But at least I'll get to see you a minute and maybe we can have lunch! I think some of your bad luck is rubbing off on me! Ugh! I'm going to try and get some sleep since it's an early flight. I'll call in the morning. I guess your phone's dead, I tried calling a couple times. Sorry if this is an inconvenience for you, but I need to get to work and back. I wish I could stay longer. This will be a tease! But then it will only be two more weeks till I fly down and stay a few days. Sweet dreams, I love you!"

I was hoping he would sleep all night and not see my message until in the morning, so that maybe I could get some sleep also. I knew if he saw the message he would be calling, no matter what time it was. As much as I tried, I couldn't get much sleep anyways, I was on edge. Tossing and turning was an understatement.

Chapter 18

(One Way Ticket)

It was June 1st, and I was up early checking on my plane status. It said my flight was cancelled! Did I read that right? I needed to get my truck. ASAP. I looked on-line at the airlines and there were plenty of seats, so I decided I'd take my chances and go straight to the airport. When my Uber didn't show, I was wondering what happened. I went to check on that too, and noticed I put PM instead of AM. Annoyed, I cancelled that reservation and luckily another one came within minutes. I needed to pull myself together. It was early, about 4am. I had little sleep, but I needed to get to the airport early to purchase a ticket, since the flight I wanted was leaving at 6am.

It felt like I was in a movie. At first it seemed to be a love story, but then all of a sudden it turned into a thriller/horror movie. How do people live like this? I had never been in any kind of deranged relationship or much drama in my life. This was all just insane and foreign to me. I should have been super tired and exhausted, but I was wide awake thanks to my adrenaline kicking into overdrive.

As soon as I got to the airport, I jumped in line hoping to purchase a one-way ticket to Key West. While waiting, my phone started blowing up. I didn't answer it since I was almost to the counter. Chad kept calling again, and again, and again. As irritating as that was, I wasn't going to answer until I was all checked in. That just got my blood flowing at full speed.

When I made it to the counter, I told the lady a little of what was going on and that I needed to get on the first flight to Key West. She said of course but had no clue on how to print out a ticket. When she saw the flight, she said there were plenty of seats. Since it was within twenty four hours of the flight taking off, I wasn't able to purchase it on-line. After some assistance, she figured out how to print out my ticket. I was lucky it was a small airport.

I was then able to text Chad, "Good morning. I'll call in a minute. I'm at the airport checking in."

He replied right away, "I'm guessing this is your way of breaking up with me. This kills me. I am so fucked now. I can't comprehend how I let myself get into this mess. My mind is racing at a mile a second now. I had the ducks in a row to make everything right again. Now I'm fucked. I should've never taken my boat out of Key West. I should've never broken all my ties for the move. A lot I should've never done that now I'm just fucked all the way around. Great way to get rid of someone though. I thought this would've worked out better. You got what you wanted. I wish I had a little notice of this. I wouldn't have destroyed myself in the process. Fuk." (RED FLAG)

Wow! So, because I needed my truck back, he was freaking out? I never said anything about breaking up, either. He said I got what I wanted? What was that supposed to mean? I was letting him use my truck and I paid for so much, I wondered what it was he thought I wanted. Honestly, it sounded like he destroyed himself. I never asked him to sail up to me in the first place. I was speechless for a minute. He was showing his true colors; true colors I did not like. I couldn't get to Key West soon enough. I just wanted my truck back and to get the hell away from him.

I replied and said, "Omg! I'm not doing this to make your life miserable. I gave my heart and soul to you! I love you! I wasn't coming down there to break up, I Just need my truck back, so I have a vehicle to get around in. I don't understand why we still can't work. I was planning on coming back in a few weeks."

I was able to call Chad just before boarding the plane and I think he finally calmed down some. I had to explain that this was not a breakup trip. I told him I would be landing at 11am and he said he would be there.

Just before take-off, I texted all three of my daughters telling them that I loved them. I didn't let them know what was going on or where I was going because I didn't want to worry them. I was so scared, and I wasn't so sure what I was up against. If Chad found out that I knew the real him, what would he do? Is he dangerous? Would he hurt me? Was there any truth to anything that he told me? Could someone really be that dishonest? Did he fake everything? Did he even like me? Surely some of our moments were real, or were they? Most of these questions might never get answered, and that hurt. My brain needed a rest. I closed my eyes while flying to Miami for a short layover before the final flight to Key West.

While waiting for my next flight in the airport, the flight to Key West from Miami, I called Sarah, my friend from Alabama. Before I was able to tell her what was happening, I started crying. It was like a faucet turned on. Once it started, I had a hard time shutting it off. I was shaking like it was twenty degrees in the airport. After finally getting out what was going on, Sarah told me to take a deep breath, get my shit together and to focus. I needed to play the game and get my truck back. That was the goal. I agreed and thanked her for listening and for helping me pull myself back up. I could fall apart later. At that moment I needed to be strong and stick with the plan.

I was halfway there. I made it this far and Chad said he would be there when I landed. That was a positive thing. He could have taken my truck and ran it off the road or into the ocean, especially if he was that hostile when he thought we were breaking up. What would he have done if I really did break up with him? What was his plan? What was his end game? All of the unknowns were making me delirious.

I was getting texts from my friends who had me on their trackers. They were checking in and making sure I was okay. I had a great team backing me up the whole way. My team consisted of a few friends from Alabama and all my friends I've made in Florida. It felt good that they were all on my side. My Florida friends have seen me glowing and excited to retire from the medical field to live on a boat since January. They

214

heard my stories of how great Chad was and how we were going to make a great team together. I had invited all of them to visit us on the boat in St. Augustine when we were planning on living there. Then it turned into them visiting us in Marathon. None of that would ever happen. I was very thankful for their support and not judging me for my bad choices and mistakes. They knew I needed their friendship at that time more than ever. I didn't have the heart to tell my family and worry them, so I was glad I had the most wonderful friends watching out for me. I also had God guiding me each step of the way. I was talking to him more than ever, praying that it would all end well.

After what seemed like a lifetime, the plane finally landed in Key West. My stomach was in knots and my legs were weak. I needed to stay focused to complete the mission I was on. A mission to get my truck back, the truck I bought eight months ago that I just paid off. I wasn't about to let some con man take that from me. He already took my heart and broke it into a million pieces.

As all of us passengers were walking into the airport, straight ahead, staring at me was the man I thought I knew and loved. Chad wasn't the same person. He had an old t-shirt on with shorts and flip flops. He looked rough and weathered, like he hadn't slept in days. Even worse, Chad looked as if he was about to lose it, like his life was spinning out of control. With no expression, no hug, no kiss, he just handed me my keys. It was the most unsettling feeling knowing what I knew about this man and pretending that I was clueless. I felt like his eyes could see right through me; they were that piercing.

He finally said, "Here's your keys like you wanted. The truck is across the street in the parking garage."

I said, "Thank you, and I'm sorry I had to come get it, but I needed a way to get back and forth to work."

He didn't say anything and since I had no luggage, we went straight for the truck.

As soon as we got in the truck he said, "I know this is the last time I'm going to see you, I know what you're doing, you are seeing someone."

I replied, "No, I've been working overtime and I'm not breaking up with you, I just need my truck."

He said, "You can let me out anywhere, I have nothing now. I had to quit a job I just got at the pet store. I should have never left Key West. I should have listened to my gut."

"It's not my fault," I said.

"I know it isn't, I don't blame you if you did find someone else, I have nothing else to offer you. I have nothing," he said with a straight face.

I drove us around, all the while trying to think about how I'd be if I was still his girlfriend and didn't know anything. So, I couldn't just drop him off anywhere. As calm as I could, I kept asking where he

216

wanted to be let out at. We were going in circles; or at least my head was. I just wanted this man out of my truck; he was scaring me. I finally stopped at a gas station, and I went inside to use the bathroom and to get us each a coke. He stayed outside smoking a cigarette while waiting for me. I was hoping he would have been gone when I came out of the gas station. I gave him the coke and he said he didn't want it. We got back in the truck and went driving around again. It was getting ridiculous, he needed to get out.

He said, "Just let me out anywhere, here, the Taco Bell parking lot."

I pulled into the Taco Bell parking lot, rounded the building and instead of parking, I stopped in the middle, just before exiting. Nobody was in front of me or behind me.

When I get nervous, I just start talking. I said, "I still plan on coming down in June as planned, we will be fine. I wasn't panning on breaking up with you. You will be fine."

"I know I will, I always do. I just had plans to take the truck in to get it serviced, now I have to cancel that. I can't work for the prison now, and I will have to let them know at the pet store I can't make it. I was doing all this for us," Chad said. "I can't go to the boat without food and be stranded there either. I guess I will stay in the mangroves." He added, "Please don't let another man wear my clothes that I left at your house. Or give them away."

I had no idea what to do. All I really wanted was for him to open up that door and get out. This person I was talking to was definitely not the person I fell in love with; he was different. Everything was different.

A car pulled up behind me and Chad was going to have to get out or we would be driving around some more. I really needed to get going on my eight hour drive back to Gainesville. I was expecting him to understand that and get out. He did. I told him bye and that I loved him, and I would see him in a few weeks. I'm not sure how much of that he believed. It didn't matter at that time, because as soon as he shut the door, I was free. I left him there on the corner of the Taco Bell parking lot with nothing, looking like a local homeless person. I didn't even offer him any money which I was proud of. It felt like a huge weight was lifted. I did it! I got my truck! I could finally breathe, even though I was still shaking, and my heart was still racing.

Not even five minutes after I drove away, Chad called. I answered, still trying my best to keep up the girlfriend façade. He said, "The gas is cheaper on the way out of town, by the way."

I looked down and I was thirty miles until empty. Of course, there wasn't any gas. I told him thank you and hung up.

Chad calls me another five minutes later to tell me that he called the guy at the Sheriff's department, where he was going to get a job doing security. He

218

said the guy got mad at him when he told him that he wouldn't be able to work there, and the guy hung up on him (RED FLAG). I didn't know what to say except that I was sorry.

Then I asked, "Can I stop at the boat to get a few things?"

He said, "Yes, the boat is unlocked. They have cameras everywhere, so I don't have to worry about anyone stealing anything."

"And my bike?" I asked.

He paused, then said, "It's not there."

I was floored. He got rid of my bike. I knew he probably pawned it or sold it, which made me sick. It was gone after just four days of being there. I should not have been surprised, but I was. I just sat there in silence because it shocked me, and I didn't know what to say.

He quickly responded with, "You can take my bike, I'll text you the code."

We hung up again. I was so angry. My bike was gone. He got rid of my bike. I loved that bike; it was given to me and was the perfect size. It had a cup holder and a place for my phone and everything. My vision started to blur some and my breathing became shallow. I needed to get out and get some fresh air. I happened to come upon a small market of local crafts and vegetables, so I stopped and got out.

The first thing I did was take a deep breath. I remembered we put some of my stuff in the backseat of Red, I looked, and nothing was there but the cooler. I then decided to check the truck bed. All the stuff I sent with him to be put on the boat was in the bed of the truck all tossed around, when, we originally put most of it in the back seat of the cab of the truck. There were empty gas cans, a duffle bag full of wet clothes, the trailer-hitch-cover my brother made me, a couple tools, and some other odds and ends. It's like he had no care about my stuff. Everything was all scattered. I shut the tailgate and needed to walk around a minute or two to get my head straight.

After getting back in the truck I noticed a few texts I missed from some girlfriends. They were so worried because to them it looked like I was in the ocean on the tracker since I had ocean on both sides of the road. Their minds were thinking I was thrown overboard and that I was in the ocean! That did kind of make me laugh a little. I told them I was okay, and I just had to stop to get some air. I let them know I was headed to the marina to get some stuff off the boat, just in-case it still looked like I was in the ocean.

I pulled into the marina where the boat was. Taking a couple more deep breaths, I got out and tried to work fast. I took his gas tank and duffle bag to the boat; I didn't want them. I had hoped the neighbors that I met would be there, but there was no sign of them. There was nobody around, which I was thankful for since I might have looked suspicious. I walked as fast as I could to the boat. There was no plank to walk over onto the boat from the dock. I thought now this is going to be interesting. Deciding to go for it, I took off my sandals and jumped. I made it, easier than I thought. I crawled down into the boat, and immediately I noticed the musty smell and all the rubbish everywhere.

The inside of the boat looked as if nobody had been on there in a while, and I could barely see the floor. It was not getting fixed up or cleaned up at all. I had to move blankets and a foam mattress topper to get to the bin I wanted. From the bin, I took out the sign I had made him with our last names on it. It wasn't even the last name he was using. The last name I used on our sign was an alias, one he hadn't used in quite some time. I should have broken it, but I was in a hurry and wasn't thinking straight. I left some clothes, kitchen stuff, and snorkel gear I wish I would have grabbed that I had forgotten about until later. I did notice one of my beach chairs on the deck, so I grabbed it. Since there was no plank over the water, I had to toss everything I wanted from the boat onto the dock, and then hoping it would make it. Out of everything I tossed, only an ashtray that I made on a spinning wheel broke. I didn't smoke anyway, so it wasn't a terrible loss. I kept it for company. Still, I was a little sad it broke because I made it myself.

After loading everything onto my truck, I noticed Chad's bike. It seemed decent enough to take. I checked my texts to see if he really did send the code for the lock, and he did! I put it in the back with the other stuff that didn't matter if it got wet. I grabbed my cooler in the back seat and opened it. The smell about knocked me over. It was the food I had sent with him four days earlier, floating in warm water. Why had he not emptied it out? What on earth was he doing all day? Was he just driving around all day doing nothing? I was so confused. There were too many questions unanswered.

I took care of the water and food and again noticed no one around. It was interesting that nobody was hanging around the marina, while I was taking stuff from the boat. I'm sure someone would have stopped me and asked questions if they did see me. It was a little after lunchtime, so maybe everyone was just out eating or stayed at work or something. Is this what real boat life looked like, not being on the boat all day like I thought? It was a little eerie, being the only one around with nothing but the sound of waves and birds to keep you company.

Finally, I was back on the road. It felt good to be back in Red: it felt comfortable, like home. It was my personal space and a place that was just mine. I was so happy I got her back. The next seven hours wouldn't be so bad, I was free.

A little while after I left, I received a text from Chad saying, "Can you open the engine room door and see if there is any water in there? If you're still there, if not, no worries. I'll be there tomorrow for a bit."

"I'm not there, sorry." I really just wanted to be left alone at that point.

222

At that same time Chad replied to me, my daughter had called me. We had a quick talk, mostly because she wanted to tell me something important. She told me some bad news about my nephew when Chad texted back.

"Ok, no prob. Did you get the bike? I sent the combo," he said.

I replied, "Yes, I did. I've been on the phone with my daughter, we just found out some bad news about their cousin, so I really don't feel like talking right now."

He said, "I'm sorry to hear that. Take your time. Breathe."

I didn't talk to or text Chad the rest of the night. After hearing the bad news, I was so distraught that I took a wrong turn, which added another hour and a half to my drive.

While driving, I decided to call Cookie and tell her what was going on. I told her to not say anything or "I told you so," but to be a friend and to just listen. She said, "Of course." I told her everything. She was surprised and glad that I was okay.

Then my parents called asking what I was doing. I was trying to avoid telling the whole story to them, but Mom knew something was up. She could tell there was something wrong with me in my voice and told me to spill it. So, I told them everything. They were shocked, and glad that I was okay also. I hate them worrying about me, even though I know they do all the time. It doesn't matter how old you get; your parents still worry.

After getting off the phone with my mom and dad, I get another call. This time it was the marina. I didn't answer. I knew what they wanted. They needed the rent money for the month of June. I listened to the voicemail that came up a minute after the call ended. They were asking if I knew how to get ahold of Chad...for the next month's rent. If that call didn't pertain to me, then I needed to disregard the message. So that's what I did. I disregarded it. I knew that was going to happen, and I was glad I had cut up the credit card that was on file there.

Another look at my phone and I noticed a message from the anonymous person who sent me that tip through messenger. I opened the message, and they were asking if I'd like to talk, and they gave me their number. Soon I would finally find out who that person was. I had an idea, but I was not certain.

It was almost 9:00pm when I pulled into the apartment. I locked up the bike, brought my stuff in, and didn't wait any longer to call that number given to me.

It was who I thought it was. It was the Canadian on the boat, named Stella, who needed a ride to Miami. She was in Canada with her boyfriend. Stella and her boyfriend were talking to me on speaker. After a few minutes of small talk, she said she was cheated out by Chad for a total of $2,445.50.

That was the money she needed for her surgery. She paid $2,145.50 for the towing fee, and Chad also had made her top off the gas tank on the boat before they left, which was $300.00. I was baffled, because he had told me that it cost him $1,600.00 to fill it up.

Curiosity got the better of me, and I later looked up the size of the boat, how big the gas tank would be, and roughly how much that would cost. It was about $350.00. Chad had never spent $1,600.00 on gas. Instead, he had Stella fill it up, for less than a quarter of that cost.

Stella said Chad had promised to give everyone on the boat $1,000.00 each when they got to St. Augustine for helping him sail the boat up. She also mentioned how angry he would get when things didn't go as planned, that he had a temper.

I listened to everything Stella and her boyfriend said. I was in disbelief, but I knew they were telling me the truth. All the tension in my gut finally unraveled itself. You can't make that shit up. She told me that Chad was known in Key West for manipulating and abusing women. He was no longer able to work at Sloppy Joe's anymore because he was harassing the waitresses. The stories just kept getting worse. This was the man I was going to live with! I wish I would have known all this information months ago. I wish I had been warned. I wish I had noticed all the signs, and paid attention to my gut feelings more. All the red flags that I now see while writing this book seem so obvious. I felt stupid, relieved, and sick to my stomach all at once.

Stella told me all kinds of stories. Apparently, Chad was mean to everyone. She kept going and told me that Chad was seeing a red-headed woman on a regular basis. Stella said she even walked up to Chad while he was kissing on some woman. Overall, Chad was a bad person, and she wanted to make sure that I didn't get myself in too deep. Stella said that I was too good of a person to be with him.

I was thankful for that, and as we were still talking about stories, I remembered what Chad had said about her. I told her that Chad had said she dropped some silver of his in the ocean, stole Chad's money jar, and even broke the toilet handle. Stella was in disbelief then, but not surprised. She said the silverware was your normal Walmart stuff and a couple pieces fell in the ocean as she was cleaning up his mess in the kitchen. Chad knew she dropped a couple pieces in the ocean, and he said it was okay.

Stella never took any money, and the toilet handle was already broken and the piece that he needed was probably less than $50.00. Nothing compared to the $2,445.50 that Chad took from her.

The story of the storm was one thing that did happen, though. Stella said she had also gotten sick with carbon monoxide and couldn't leave the bedroom because she was so weak. She mentioned how scary the storm was, and that they all really thought they would not make it. Chad never mentioned to me that anyone else was sick; just him.

Stella also mentioned how Chad was telling her that when he got up to St. Augustine, he would be committed to only me, as he winked at her. They both knew that he was with other women. Whether they all knew about each other was still a mystery to Stella.

Everything I was hearing seemed too much for my brain to comprehend, and seconds seemed to take hours. Thinking back, Chad told me he was faithful from the day we met, that he never needed anyone but me. He always said how much he wanted to be with me, how he was "all in" and was so excited about our future. Wow, I was such a fool to believe him. I trusted him.

There was so much information in such a short amount of time. My mind was numb, and my body was exhausted. I needed to get some sleep. I thanked Stella for telling me everything, and we both decided to keep in touch before hanging up. I knew she was a good person when I had met her through FaceTime. Even with what Chad had told me about her before, I never did get a "bad" vibe from Stella, even on the phone. Chad had lied about her, trying to get me to believe that she was an awful person. It was all the opposite, though.

The next morning after waking up, I noticed a text message from Chad at 3:50am saying, "Hope all is well in your world. Have a good day today."

A few hours later at 6:09am, he asks, "What are your plans for the day?"

I had told him multiple times that I had to get back to work, did he ever even listen to anything I said? I wanted to tell him everything Stella told me. Anger was taking a hold of me, but I took my time to think about what I was going to say. I knew that was going to be my last text to him.

At 8:53am, I texted back saying, "My plans are to tell you to stop with this act of yours, stop pretending to be someone you're not! I know who you are and who you're not! You were never a ranger for 20yrs, was discharged from the coast guard for psychological reasons, a warrant for your arrest in February, bank robbery, in jail, on probation, etc. etc.! You're a pathological liar and manipulative and I can't believe I fell for it! I should have seen the signs earlier. You can't work at Sloppy Joe's because you harass the waitresses, and you have a red head woman you see on a regular basis! You're a piece of shit and have nothing! You get everyone to pay your fees without paying them back! I'm sure you even sold my bike! It makes me sick that I introduced you to my family, friends and even around my grandson! I have a huge weight lifted knowing I got out of a bad situation and glad I caught on but not soon enough! I gave you way more than you ever deserved! Don't try contacting me or I will call the cops and have your fucking nasty ass thrown in jail! Again, that's my plans for today!"

I watched my phone until the message sent, took a breath, then I blocked him. That was it. I couldn't believe those last few days. What a whirlwind. There was still so much racing through my mind. Some of it was starting to make sense, why he

228

said certain things or didn't do certain things. How could I have been so blind? I kept asking myself how did I not see the red flags? Love. Love will do that to you.

That afternoon I got another phone call from the marina. They left a message saying that the credit card on file was not going through. So, I decided to call them back and tell them what I knew. First of all, I told them I was just helping a friend. Secondly, Chad's last name was not his last name and to look him up on-line. They said, "Oh, hell!" They ended up telling me that he was not allowed back on the boat because he didn't have the correct paperwork.

That made sense as to why he was not in a hurry to get back there, and why he kept on going into Key West instead of stopping at the marina in Marathon. He had a place to stay at the apartments, whomever that was.

While cleaning out Red, I noticed a picture was missing of me and my daughter that I had in the visor. I felt around in the pocket it was in, and it was there, but facing backwards. I put it back where I wanted it. As I was vacuuming, there were some short hairs in the back seat, as if a dog had been sitting there. I knew then that Chad had let a random woman with a dog in my truck. He hid everything that was mine. That's why my trailer-hitch-cover my brother made me was off. I found out later from Stella that he told everyone on the island that it was his truck. It made me mad to think that he used my truck as not just a means to get around, but to pick up other women. The only good thing was he took good care of Red, and I was thankful for that. He could have destroyed her.

I still had a couple days of work before I was flying back to Alabama for my daughter's bridal shower. It had been one crazy week, and it would definitely take some time to process it all. I was able to focus on work while there, but during my breaks and at Julia's apartment my mind couldn't keep up with everything Stella told me.

I posted a tidbit on Facebook at how I had recently watched the Tinder Swindler on Netflix, and I couldn't believe how those girls could be so foolish by willingly giving away money to that guy, but there I was, doing the same thing. The only difference was I was doing it in person. I was out almost $7,000.00 and most of it I willingly gave or paid for stuff. He only asked for the marina fees. He didn't even ask to use my truck, and he didn't want me selling my house, even though he joked about it once in a while. He was good and knew how to work it.

My friend Casey (the one who took Cookie and I out on the pontoon boat) saw my post and wanted to interview me on her podcast. I told her I needed a few weeks to process everything and get my facts straight. Until then, I needed to go celebrate my daughter at her wedding shower in Alabama.

Chapter 19

(Not Over)

My flight home to Alabama was quiet, except for my mind. I rehashed everything during my whole relationship with Chad. It was unbelievable. I was at a loss. So much had happened from the start, and I had all those gut feelings telling me something wasn't right, but I ignored them all, along with ignoring my friends. I couldn't help but feel stupid and sorry for myself, but I also knew I couldn't keep beating myself up. All I needed to do was focus on my daughter and her wedding coming up. It was going to be a wonderful time and that's what mattered most.

I arrived early to Alabama on a Saturday, so I decided to go to the pool. My neighborhood friends were there, and I started telling them my story about me and Chad while having a few drinks. One of them asked what the movie was called I was talking about. The movie I was talking about was mine. My real life movie. It was still hard to believe. Everyone was intrigued. I guess I would have been, too, if I hadn't just lived it.

That evening my daughter and her fiancé were staying with me at my house while they were in town. When I started to tell her about Chad, I broke down and cried. All my emotions I had been holding in just came out like a flood. I bawled and sobbed all over her shoulder. I was telling her how sorry I was, that I didn't know. I felt so bad, especially since her shower was the next morning. She comforted me like I was the child. What a wonderful daughter I raised. She was there for me when I should have been the one there for her, the night before her bridal shower. Sometimes emotions can control you instead of the other way around. I was really glad my daughter was there for me. She handled it like a pro.

The bridal shower was nice, and everyone had a good time. I knew what I had to do when it ended. When I got back home, I threw away all the clothes Chad had left. It was time to get rid of him for good. He left a bin full of other odds and ends that I sorted through, but not much was worth keeping. I did keep the coral he found, and placed it on my porch, which fit since my porch was beach themed. Plus, I'm sure it was stolen. I didn't think you could even sell coral. From the other stuff Chad left behind, I kept a standup fan for my garage, and a nice lightweight jacket that would be good for work. It wasn't easy getting rid of the past year, but it was something I needed to do.

After sorting through all the stuff that was Chad's, I felt a lot better. I felt good about keeping the small things I kept; he got rid of my bike and lied to me about a lot of things. With less weight on my shoulders, it was time to get back to work in Florida.

After arriving back at the apartment, I wanted to find out more about Chad, so I did my own research. I found on Instagram the girl that had the restraining order against him, her name was Sherry. Chad had stolen money from her, too. I reached out to her asking if there was more to add about him. She replied, "Yes there is!" She said she would call me, but I never heard from her.

I reached out to my new friend Bailey from the marina in Marathon that I thought I'd be living at. I told her what happened and why Chad and I wouldn't be living there. Just like my other friends in Alabama, she was blown away with how insane everything was. Bailey told me she hadn't seen Chad since he left for Disney. Her and her boyfriend, Derrick, had suspicions about Chad, and even wondered when he was going to move his boat before they redid the docks. They hardly ever saw him at the marina. Instead, Chad would leave Jerry on the boat with no food. Jerry was a nice guy and a hard worker, working on the boat almost every day she saw him. Bailey said she never saw Chad do anything to the boat, and after he left for Disney, he never came back. It was my turn to be dumbfounded.

Bailey and I still talked often and had a good time chatting, so we spoke about plans for the near future. It turns out we both like to ride bikes and go for runs. She was going to teach me all about my Go-Pro and how to start a YouTube channel when we met. Before everything happened, Bailey had also been looking forward to having a friend there in Marathon.

A few days later, Bailey told me that after listening to my story, it made her take a good look at her own relationship with Derrick. She said they were going through a rough patch, but after listening to me, they opened up and started talking more. Bailey mentioned about how she and Derrick were working things out and listening to me really helped. She told me to do the podcast and to tell my story, because if it helped her relationship, it could help others, too.

That made me feel good, like I was meant to tell my story about Chad. If life has taught me anything, it's that your experiences can help others through their experiences. It's sad that some of our life moments and stories are not pleasant ones. Everyone gets hurt at some point, and no one said life was going to be easy. However, how we deal with our hurt is what matters, and this experience wasn't going to stop me from all the good my life has to offer in the future.

My mind constantly combed back through all of mine and Chad's conversations and texts. I was able to start sorting out what was real and what wasn't. Rereading some texts, I was able to catch some of the points where he lied, and even saw how awful he was to me. How could he be so mean? I just wanted us to have a genuine life full of fun and love. What did he see in me that made me a target? All of this was fuming in me. I couldn't help myself, I had to send a text message.

On June 12th, I said, "I want to add how awful it is that you play with people's feelings and emotions! You don't give a shit about anyone or anything, but yourself! You lie about how you feel to get your way! I let my wall down and put my heart on the line for you and you couldn't care less. People work hard to get where they are and it's tough to get back on track when they help someone they trust and possibly love,

234

then never get the help back in return. You take money, you take feelings, you take, take and take! If you ever worked hard in your life you'd understand. You'd rather steal from others than make your own way. You steal everything…hearts, emotions, $. 'I've been faithful since the day we met!' What bullshit! I can't believe I believed that! I was so stupid! You've hurt me too many times and this was the last. Not everyone is cruel like you, I will meet my real soulmate someday…while I'm out traveling the world. I just hope you realize all the pain you cause and hope you can change and not continually hurt others. You need help."

I wasn't sure if he was even going to get that message or not, but it felt good to send it.

After thinking it through, I went through with the podcast, reliving the past year. If it helps one person to get out of a dangerous relationship by noticing the red flags, then it was all worth it. I was so nervous being on camera, but I did it, and it felt good. The feeling of being proud of yourself is one of the best feelings in the world, and I walked out of that room with a sense of great satisfaction.

June was a busy month, and it flew by. I had my moments of breakdowns. Going from talking or texting Chad almost every day and planning a future together, to nothing. It was extremely hard to swallow at times. I felt lonely some days, while other days I felt free and better than okay. It was hard on the day I was supposed to be flying to Key West that month, and that hurt because it felt like Chad was still taking

235

my money. As time went on, I became more okay with myself, even throughout the rest of the year. In the end, I knew everything was going to turn out for the best.

I signed another contract at the hospital I was working at in Florida for thirteen more weeks which would start after I took five weeks off. During those five weeks, I had a trip to Seattle planned, then the wedding, and picking up a little job at the hospital in Alabama that I had left at the beginning of the year. July was going to be just as busy as June was. It would be good to have positive things to look forward to.

My trip to Seattle was great, besides the empty seat next to me on the plane where Chad was supposed to be. That was more money lost and wasted. The peace and quiet experience was better than the lies he told me though. My daughter's wedding in South Alabama was beautiful, and before I knew it, my five week vacation was over. It was time to get back to Florida for another thirteen-week assignment. Luckily enough, Julia signed another thirteen-week assignment, also, and we decided to stay roommates in the apartment she was renting. I was happy about that. In a time when everything was changing, I was glad something was staying the same.

I was so busy for the month of July that I didn't have time to dwell on the fact that I had rearranged my future, and then was rearranging everything back. During my eight hour drive back to Florida from

236

Alabama, my emotions and thoughts were all over the place. It was like starting over; like I didn't know where I belonged anymore. That was when my mind would catch up on what I had processed and let my feelings out. What once used to be a drive I enjoyed was now something I was dreading. I knew then that it was time to figure out where I was supposed to be after the next thirteen weeks.

It was August 8th, and I was pulling into the apartment building in Florida. As I was unloading and walking up the steps, I noticed my bike (the bike Chad told me to take) was missing. I had it secured to the railing with the chain lock, the same lock Chad gave me the combination to. The two other bikes had not been touched; they were still in the same place. My heart instantly dropped. The only other person who knew the combination was Chad. If someone was going to steal it, they would have cut the lock and left it laying on the ground, or just taken the other bikes. Plus, the people that lived in the apartment building were the only people that knew where the bikes were. The bikes were not easily noticeable under the stairway.

I instantly called Julia, who was in Tennessee visiting her family, to ask her if she noticed anything. She said the bike was there when she left four days ago. That made me very uneasy. Chad did have an uncle who was only twenty minutes away, who he may have convinced to drive over to get it. It made me look over my shoulder every time I went outside.

I decided to message Sherry from Instagram. I asked her if she thought he might be dangerous.

She replied right back and said, "Yes, I do very much so. He was abusive to his ex. And as you know very-much-a-liar. The story Chad told was much different than her story when I met her in person months later. I would tread lightly. I don't think he would outright hurt you, but I do think that he will try to make your life hell!"

That made me super nervous. During the month of June, I felt uneasy and kept checking to make sure the bike was still there. I had thoughts that he would be waiting on the steps when I got in from work any given day. There was a feeling of being followed. I thought that the uneasy feelings and looking over my shoulders would have been gone at that point, and it was for a short time, but it was back, just a couple months later into August. I felt the same way when I went home to Alabama, wondering if he was going to come and take the coral back that was sitting on my back porch. Not that he even had a vehicle to get around in, but I'm sure he could swindle someone into taking a road trip with him.

I was thinking that in his mind I am the person at fault that ruined his life. He had given everything up for me and look at what I did. That's what narcissists do: they turn everything around on the innocent to make them feel like the victims.

I racked my brain trying to figure out what his end game was. Did he ever have feelings for me?

Was everything a lie? Where was he now? What was he doing? What happened to the boat? So many questions. The more I played our conversations in my head the more I saw all the red flags. It definitely was too good to be true, but there I was, going for it.

After a few days I started to relax some, until I got a message on August 14th. It was from Sherry. Sherry shared a screenshot of a message she received. It said, "Hey girl? This is probably a long shot, but my boyfriend has somehow gotten wrapped up with Chad… and we believe he is trying to con us out of a sailboat that his dad left him when he passed away. He's been dealing with Chad's shady ass for some time now and the entire situation is sketchy. I looked up his arrest records and found a theft of property where you were the victim. Can you tell me a little more about Chad? Thank you, my name is Clare."

In the screenshot Sherry replied, "Don't trust him. Don't buy it. He let me rent an apartment that wasn't his, gave me a key that didn't work and took all my money. I was new in town, so it was literally all I had!"

Sherry was messaging me asking for my take on it, and wanted to ask me first before she gave Clare my name. I told her that was fine, that Clare could get ahold of me, and I'd answer any questions she had.

This was still not over. I had someone wanting to find out more about Chad from me, and it sounded like it wasn't even his boat! I was staying with him on a stolen boat! I was on a stolen boat by myself one day, too. He was sailing up on a stolen boat! He mentioned a few times we could sell it and buy something else. Wow. That was so unbelievable. What was he planning on doing with me and him on a stolen boat? My mind was blown. Here I was trying to move on. Hearing from these girls was making it very difficult to move forward. But maybe I could get some answers finally.

I couldn't wait to hear from Clare, the girlfriend of the son whose father owned the boat and committed suicide. At least that was what Chad had told me.

The next day at work I received a message, "Hey Niki Rae! I got your info from Sherry. I am Sam's girlfriend Clare and we just got back from Key West today. We went to go check out Sam's dad's boat (Chad was looking after it) and we were so upset when we got there. The inside was disgusting, the dinghy was halfway sunk, and he is claiming he has twenty grand invested in the boat and that there were receipts on board. A couple neighbors told us other people were staying on it as well. He also sold Sam's Dad's moped. I did a deep dive into him, and he sounds like a con artist and a dangerous man. Do you know anything about the boat and what Chad may have been saying. He told a few people it was his boat."

My mouth dropped. I was shocked about

everything. It was all so crazy. Chad told me it was his boat, his scooter, his car, everything was all his. Unbelievable. If what Clare said was true, the scooter wasn't even his! All Chad told me was lies. The sad part was that I actually believed everything Clare said in her message. I couldn't wait until I had a moment to talk to Clare and Sam and find out all about what they knew. My shift at work couldn't end quick enough.

After too long a shift at the hospital, I was finally back at the apartment and able to call Clare and Sam. We dove straight into it. They told me that ten months ago when they found out Sam's dad died, they went to Key West to check out the boat his dad lived on. Sam met Chad then, and Chad said he would keep an eye on the boat for them while they sorted things out. Sam and Clare had no idea that Chad had moved onto the boat, was going to sail it up to St. Augustine, and possibly sell it. They asked if I knew where the scooter was. I told them unfortunately, he pawned it. Sam and Clare were so disgusted at the whole thing. After recently locating their boat, they had it taken to a dry dock to get it worked on and said that Chad was not allowed anywhere near it. The boat was the only thing Sam had of his dad's, and they wanted to clean it up to possibly live on or use it as an Airbnb. They said it took a week to clean it out, it was that nasty. Chad was giving them the runaround and Sam even sent me screenshots of their messages.

They started messaging Chad on June 6th, asking him to call back or they would call the coast guard and find out where he was. Chad finally messaged back on June 7th, saying he dropped his phone and broke it, and that he was in Jersey fixing a garage that a tree fell on. Sam had told Chad to call him when he got a chance. Chad said he would be back on the boat by that weekend.

It was June 14th, when Sam tried calling Chad again with no answer, but Chad replied later saying he was driving and asked what was up. The messages then went to July 5th, when Chad was saying he got an email from the marina saying that they hoped his stay was pleasant, and so Chad asked Sam if he had moved the boat. Sam said he did not, and asked again where the boat was. Chad said the same marina in Marathon, and that he was in Jersey dealing with the deaths of his brother and sister from a drunk driver that hit them head on.

The next message was August 8th, when Sam was on the boat and telling Chad how nasty it was, and if he wanted to keep anything off of it to let him know. Chad replied saying he locked it up when he left. I knew that was a lie because Chad told me he didn't have to lock it up due to all the cameras at the marina. It must have been exhausting trying to keep up with all the lies he told everyone. I wouldn't be able to keep anything straight with how many stories he made up to every other person.

Chad asked Sam how much he was going to sell the boat for, because Chad spent about 20k on the boat. Chad wanted to know what the buyout would be. Sam said he wasn't sure if he was going to even sell, because that was his father's boat and that's all

Sam had left of his dad. Also, Sam wondered where the 20k went since the boat looked worse off than when he left it, and there was no proof or documentation that anything had been done, altered, or fixed. He said the boat was basically destroyed since the last time he saw it along with the dinghy halfway sunk.

Chad said the receipts were on board for the stuff he did, and that he got hit by a storm with no damage to the inside of the boat. He added that he could put the boat at a marina down in Key West and take her over. He said if there was any damage from other people then that was on the marina, not himself. He kept saying he could get a slip for the boat in Key West.

A couple days went by and Sam messaged Chad telling him that he was getting the boat hulled out and fixed up. There was a lot of water damage from a leaking window. Sam also found a lot of drug paraphernalia all over and heard that a couple was staying on it for a few weeks. Chad replied saying he was in Miami, and if people were living on it at a secured marina, then that's on them. Sam was trying to find out from Chad when all the damage was done, who was on it, and when, for the adjuster. Chad just kept giving him the runaround with no straight answers, and said he was in meetings in Miami.

Sam and Clare were trying to put some pieces together and ended up talking to some of the locals in Key West. In the texts, Sam told Chad they had some interesting talks. Chad jumped back saying he didn't care what bullshit rumors people were saying about him; people were mad at him when he left Key West because he couldn't give anyone more money. Combined, all the people roughly owed him five grand. He added that when Sam leaves the island the same people will talk about him as well, and that they probably already had a story made up going around. Chad mentioned he was in Ft. Lauderdale at a three day conference and wouldn't be available to talk much the rest of the time.

So, if he was really in Jersey, Miami, and Ft. Lauderdale, then that means that he could have taken the bike that I had chained up while he was passing through. But then again, that could all be lies, too.

How many times had he ignored me for a day when he was hanging out at the apartment where his "fishing buddy" lived? He was probably sitting on a curb or in the mangroves in Key West while texting Sam. Chad was the kind of person, I was finding out, that absolutely did not want to take responsibility or accountability to anything. Telling sob stories or lies would be the best way to avoid getting blamed for anything that really was his fault.

Sam asked Chad again where the scooter was, and he would like it back. Chad told him he sold it to pay for the dockage fee. I knew that was a total lie since I was the one who paid the marina fees. Once again, I found myself disgusted at the audacity of that man.

244

When reading all that, I wondered what on earth went through Chad's mind. From the outside it was plain to see Chad was totally giving Sam the runaround and avoiding him, from giving vague answers to telling a lot of stories in order to shift the topics. I just couldn't help but wonder: where was he?

Clare, Sam, and I all took a breath and sat in silence for a moment, taking in everything we shared. I thanked them for telling me everything, and I was so sorry that Chad did that to them. He conned me out of a lot of money, too, and I really did think the boat was his. If I had known better, I would have tried to do something. Sam and Clare didn't blame me, and they also said they were sorry that I went through so much.

There was a pause, then Sam said to Clare, "Did you tell her?"

I said, "Tell me what?"

Clare said, "While we were cleaning out the boat, we found some pamphlets on HIV/AIDS."

My stomach did a turn in my body and my heart started pounding. When was this going to be over? What the hell! Clare said it's probably nothing, but to get checked out anyways. I was thinking maybe that was why his dad committed suicide and the pamphlets had nothing to do with Chad. Plus, I couldn't picture Chad packing pamphlets back on the boat. But it still made me sick to think there was a possibility. I couldn't think much after that. We didn't talk too much longer. We exchanged numbers and hung up.

That night I couldn't stop thinking about the what ifs. What if I had known it was a stolen boat? What if I found out sooner? What if he comes and tries to harm me because I found him out? What if he did give me AIDS, and what would I tell my girls? It made me sick. I looked up signs and symptoms, just in case. It had been three months since I had seen Chad, and I had no symptoms. Then again, I read that it could live in your body and be dormant for a while. I was definitely planning on getting checked out when I got back to Alabama. I had a hard time sleeping that night. It was a nightmare that wasn't going away.

Chapter 20

(Confrontation)

After learning about everything, my guard went back up like a brick wall. It was going to be hard to trust again, but I decided to continue to live life to the fullest and chalk this up as a lesson, even though it was a hard lesson. I would definitely be more aware when meeting people and I would not be in any hurry.

The rest of the summer I made plans with my girlfriends. We went on outings, we went on a cruise, went rafting, and explored the area around us. I also did a solo trip and rode a horse during sunset on the beach. I did lemur yoga and visited an elephant sanctuary. It was all great and it helped me to put Chad in the rearview mirror.

I also made it to the doctor's office and told him my story and that I had wanted all the tests done. I told him I was 99.9% sure that I didn't have anything, but I wanted to be 100% sure. I had all the possible tests done and checked out at 100%! I had nothing. What a relief that was. It was a weight lifted and I felt like I could finally move on. What a scare that was. One that I would not wish on anybody. It goes to show that you really cannot trust anyone and need to be careful.

In early September, Bailey from Marathon messaged me with the news that Jerry passed away. He was the homeless, harmless sweet guy that was sailing up with Chad. Jerry went up North to help a friend bring back a boat to Key West, and I guess a storm came and he didn't make it. The locals in Key West were going to have a little memorial for him at Malory Square. I hated hearing that he passed. He was such a sweet man and never asked for anything. He was a happy person and I enjoyed talking to him. I wish I could have attended the memorial. I was wondering if Chad would be there to pay his respects. I hoped he would have. Chad was like a brother to Jerry, and it was the least Chad could do after everything.

It was almost the end of both mine and Julia's contracts. She got her old job back in Nashville and I got my old job back in Alabama. We both were moving back to our homes soon. I was still going to apply for travel jobs out West to be near my parents, but I was going to stay home throughout the winter. One of my daughters was pregnant, and I wanted to be there for her and the baby. Another daughter and her son were moving in with me, also. It looked as if my place was going to be in Alabama for the time being.

Julia and I decided to take one last trip together before we both parted ways. She wanted to go to Key West, of all places! I was a little hesitant, but after some thought, I figured that might be some closure for me. Not closure in seeing Chad, but closure in knowing that not even Chad could dictate where I go. I did love Key West, after all.

Soon after deciding that's where our last trip would be, we took off to Key West. We planned to stay two nights at a decent hotel that Chad did not work at. It was the end of October, so the first part of Fantasy Fest would be going on.

My stomach felt queasy the closer we got to Key West. I was excited about being there because Key West was fun, but I was feeling anxious. The last time I was there was when I retrieved Red, my truck, and it was the last time I saw Chad. Deep down I was wondering where he was and if I'd run into him.

We came upon Marathon, and I had to show Julia the marina that I thought I was going to be living at. We walked the docks, and I showed her the slip that we had. She agreed at how nice it was and she could totally see me living there and understood why I liked it. After showing her the bathrooms, which were still just as nice, we went to get back in the truck. I noticed I didn't have my phone with me, and panic started to creep in. We backtracked where we walked and couldn't find it anywhere. All my info was on my phone. I didn't want this to be a bad start of our little get a way in Key West.

Julia called my phone a couple times with no answer. I called my daughter on Julia's phone and had her look at my phone's location. She said it was somewhere there at the marina. Julia called it again and finally someone answered. It was in the office. They said maintenance found it in the bathroom while replacing the toilet paper. I was so ecstatic and relieved! My mind instantly eased on the worst-case scenario I didn't want to think about: Chad followed me. Being back in South Florida made me uneasy and nervous overall, and I thought that may have been what caused me to be forgetful. Hopefully the nerves would die down once we made it into Key West. I wanted to have fun on this trip and not have a crazy ex ruin it.

After another hour, we made it to the hotel and checked in. The hotel was perfect and on the water. It was also just a block away from the apartments where I would see Chad at on the tracker. I didn't plan it that way, it just happened. That was all I could think about, though. How many times did I see him there? I wanted to drive by and see it, but I wasn't sure why. Curiosity, I suppose. I didn't tell Julia any of that.

We took a shuttle into town. I wanted to walk on the docks and show Julia where Chad and I would park the dinghy and go eat. She was very curious herself and wanted me to show her, which made it better and made the whole process easier on me. It was like I needed to find out some truth to what Chad did and why. I needed some answers. I did fine on my own the past few months, but then it all came back and was staring me in the face. Having Julia there willing to be part of my healing journey was such a blessing.

Walking on the docks, we ran into two of the locals that I had met with Chad. We started talking to them and they remembered who I was. I asked them why they didn't warn me. Looking a little embarrassed, they said they didn't know me very well and didn't know how bad he was then. The said Chad had conned them out of money, too. It was his eyes and charm; he knew how to work them to get what he wanted. They also mentioned the red-headed woman, and even said he was seen with a few other women that didn't look familiar, all while he was with me. My stomach felt sick.

After chatting a few minutes, the girl invited Julia and I out to their island to visit whenever we were in town again. I told Julia that they must have really liked us because not just anyone gets invited out there. It was like a little community, they all stuck together and usually did not take in outsiders. Julia had a way with people, though; she was very likable. I finally asked them if Chad was working anywhere. They seemed a little hesitant to tell me, but they did, and said to not mention them at all if I ran into him. I think they were scared of what he might do.

It made me feel a little better knowing that other people got scammed, too. Not that it was okay, and I did feel bad for them, but it made me feel that I wasn't alone. I wasn't the only one who didn't see the red flags.

We went on our way heading to Duval Street and to the famous Sloppy Joe's. After taking a seat at the bar, I noticed one of the security guys named Tom was working. He was going to be the first person to sail up to St. Augustine with Chad but bailed after he realized Chad was full of it. Tom recognized me right away and said he had so much to tell me. He didn't have time to talk since he was working, so we invited him to our hotel pool the next day. I was curious as to what he had to say about Chad.

We ended up turning in a little early that night due to Julia not feeling well. It was a long day, and we didn't eat much.

I was looking forward to a run in the morning next to the ocean, but I couldn't stop thinking about possibly running into Chad at his work and what I would say to him. All the questions I had were burning. Being back in Key West was bringing up all my feelings and it was working on me. I once loved this guy with all my heart and soul. Some things just don't go away that easy, especially when they are big feelings. During the past couple months of moving on, I was busy with work up in Gainesville, which helped keep me occupied and not get caught up in the "what ifs" and other possible scenarios, good or bad. Then I was back in Key West, within reach of the one who hurt me and broke my heart. How could I not try to confront him? Although I was the worst at confrontation, it was something I felt like had to happen. I didn't think I could leave Key West without seeing him. I had no idea it was going to feel like that. Maybe being back in Key West was not such a good idea.

The morning came and I went for a two-mile run to clear my thoughts. It didn't really help; all I could think about was what I would say to Chad when I saw him. Since I asked those locals from the night before, I knew exactly where he was working at.

After Julia and I ate breakfast, we decided to take the conch tour where you can hop on and off wherever you like, and another one would be by shortly to pick you back up where you left off. The tour gave out great history and information on everything, but my mind was not focusing on anything the driver was saying. The only information that stuck from that tour was that it was illegal to kill the chickens that roam free around Key West: you would go to jail and be fined. Out of all the history of Key West, I remembered the useless tidbits about chickens.

We hopped off at the Southernmost point in Key West to get our pictures. I was back at the place where this whole thing started. I thought about the bike I rented that day. My decision felt so good that day; I was in a new town I had always wanted to visit, by myself, on my first solo trip. Cookie would come in that evening, and that next night we saw and met Chad for the first time. Sadness, frustration, freedom, happiness, and sorrow all filled my heart.

From the Southernmost point, we started walking into town. Julia was having a good time. My heart started racing because I knew we were getting close to where Chad was working. I had an instant stomachache. That usually happens when I get nervous. What was I going to say? I still didn't know.

Coming up on Chad's work, time slowed. Here we were and as we walked around the corner, there he was.

When we rounded the corner, my legs felt like lead, but I kept walking. Chad was still working, but when he saw me, he looked straight at me without an expression, almost as if he wasn't surprised, and said, "Good to see you, Niki Rae."

It was like he was looking right through me. I was so nervous, all I mustered out was, "Well it's good to see you working."

He replied, "I've always had a job, and multiple jobs. I had a couple jobs when I met you."

I didn't know what to do, so I kept walking and said, "I'm sure you'll be scamming some other women now."

He said, "Oh whatever, I don't know where you get your information from, but it's all lies."

I kept walking and Julia stayed right beside me not saying a word. I told her I was so nervous. It was strange to see him with no expression or emotion whatsoever. His eyes were piercing. So cold. That was not the Chad I used to know. He was different. I still had questions. After we walked a few more blocks, I told Julia I had to go back and ask some questions. I couldn't leave it like that with no answers. She said to me, "You got this."

A stranger heard her and repeated, "You got this!"

I laughed and said, "Yes, I got this!"

The stranger said, "Say it louder: You got this!"

A few stores down, I yelled, "I got this!"

Everyone around was looking and smiling, encouraging me. It was a great feeling to have strangers backing you up even though they had no clue as to why.

Feeling more empowered, I went straight up to Chad telling him I had some questions to ask. Before I could stop myself, one question turned into another, and I couldn't stop. When I get nervous, I get a belly ache and I talk. I had asked why he did what he did, did he ever have feelings for me, and why would you even lie about being in the military. He told me he always loved me and that believing one of the locals was the wrong thing to do. I asked him what he was talking about, and he said the guy he got a job for at Sloppy Joe's, whatever his name was he said.

Confused, I asked, "Tom?"

He said, "Yes, you can't believe anything he says, but I hear you invited him to hang out with you. You're going to believe one person. And did you know the owners are selling the boat? I have a boat I'm renting and am starting up a business. It's out at stock island if you want to see."

Wow, so Tom apparently ran and told Chad that I was in town that fast. But, why? And I wasn't getting any answers to any of my questions. It seemed that Chad talks in circles, with not a straight answer in sight.

I said, "I'm not sure what to believe. And if I was a mean person, I'd be telling you off right now, but I'm not. And your shirt is inside out."

I definitely need a coach to help me be mean to someone, because it isn't in my DNA. All I ever do is end up saying the most unintelligent things. It's like my brain shuts down and scrambles words together and I spit them out.

I told Julia that it was time to move on. So, we ended the conversation, if that's what you even want to call it, and we moved on. I wasn't sure if I felt better or worse. It was not the closure I was thinking, but I guess it was better than none. He was never going to change, and I could see that. But we did connect at the end of the weird talk. Behind his cold eyes, deep down, I still saw the good in him, and the person I fell in love with.

Julia and I kept walking and we decided to eat at one of the restaurants on the water overlooking the dinghy docks. While eating, another one of the locals that I had met through Chad and had dinner with awhile back named Missy was walking by. I stopped her to see if she remembered me. She said yes, she does and that she didn't know how mean Chad was until recently. She said he was known in town as Cheater Chad.

I was glad I ran into the people that I had met when I was with Chad. He may not ever give me closure from himself, but it helped me to close some doors. It also helped to know that I wasn't the only one who was naïve and taken advantage of. He did a number on quite a few people.

Before returning to our hotel, we stopped in at Kermit's Key Lime Pie's, and I ordered a pie to be overnighted to my parents' house. They would finally get the pie that Chad never sent. I wished I could have been there to see their expressions when they finally received it. I left there with a smile on my face.

That next afternoon while we were hanging at the pool, Tom stopped by to talk like he said he would. I asked him if he told Chad that we were there and asked why. He said yes, he did, that he wanted to rub it in his face. Tom said he's been trying to run Chad out of town, because he is a bad man and needs to stop abusing women. He said Chad preys on older women tourists. He mentioned that when he was going to sail up with Chad, nothing was working right on the boat, and everything needed to be worked on. Tom realized then that Chad was full of it, so Tom decided to move on.

Tom told us some more stories, and it seemed that he was obsessed with Chad and trying to make Chad's life miserable. I'm not that mean of a person; I feel that people will get what they deserve eventually, and it's not my place to judge or to take things in my own hands. I wasn't sure how much I believed from Tom since I really didn't know him, and at the same time it made me feel a little sad for Chad somehow. Tom had sailed down from up north after retiring and decided to stay in Key West for a while. He said he could usually read people, but he did not read anything from Chad. When Tom finally saw Chad's true colors, he was floored. Tom agreed at how good Chad was, and he was embarrassed at how he fell for

Chad's charm. At that point, it was getting late, and Tom needed to get to work. We said our goodbyes and Tom left me and Julia at the pool with our thoughts.

That night Julia and I went out and met a couple guys that we ended up dancing with and hanging out with. They were from Chicago and seemed genuine, even though I really didn't know what that was anymore. But they helped me forget about Chad for the evening, and I had a lot of fun.

The next day Julia talked me into calling out at work, and we booked another night in our hotel. We chartered a boat and one of the guys from Chicago joined us and paid their share. We all had so much fun. I knew then that everything was going to be okay, and that life would move on. We get hurt and we get back up; it's a cycle. What matters is how we deal with the hurt. Some days I dealt with it okay, and other days I did not. I did know that time was my friend, and I was hoping It wouldn't take too long for me to feel comfortable about dating again. I left that trip with Julia feeling good about my life and moving forward overall. I was able to see Chad and not throw up, which was a definite win for me.

After leaving Key West and getting back to our apartment, I couldn't stop thinking about Chad and our conversations. I was usually fine, until I had time alone to think about him. For some reason I wanted to text him and tell him more of how I felt. The more I tried to fight it, the stronger the urge became.

On October 28th, I texted, "I'm not even sure you are going to get this, but I'm sending it anyways, just because I have a few things to say. I think at one time you really wanted to be that great person you talked about, which is the one I fell in love with, but you can't change who you really are which is a cold hearted human being. I don't know how you can sleep at night. I never talked to Tom until I ran into him at Sloppy Joe's either. He has his own issues with you, seeing me just stirred the pot, I think. I had my fill from other people about you, not just one or two either, plus all the stuff on the internet. I didn't come to Key West to see you, I came to have a good time with Julia, it just so happened I ran into you. It was closure for me though, to see you look straight through me. I'm nothing to you. I'm doing great and love my life and plan on putting you in the past, all except when we dressed up last year, which was so much fun. That's the Chad I like to remember. Maybe one day you could try and be that person you pretend to be. And one more thing…I overnighted a key lime pie from Kermit's to my parents' house while I was there since you never did. They've been eating on it."

Chad messaged back that night saying, "I'm not what you people say I am. I didn't look right through you. I loved you, Niki Rae. I didn't look through you. I wanted to hold you honestly. I can tell by your aura that you've been touched by someone else. That threw my senses off."

My anger got the best of me, and I couldn't help myself. I added, "Omg! You really are crazy! You've been unfaithful since the day we met! I've

259

been the faithful one, and for what! To get used and taken advantage of. You opened my eyes and I'm taking care of me now! I don't need anyone telling me lies and getting my hopes up, never again! I'm going to do what I want when I want, I'm going to go places and see the world!"

He replied, "Used and taken advantage of? Wtf? Who said that. I was the only one who told you not to sell anything. You've got it all wrong. I loved you every minute. I never strayed from you. Never. I don't know where you got that bullshit story from anyway. I loved you unconditionally. You had my soul. I loved every minute we spent together. Even our twelve hour ride in the truck. Lol. I wouldn't have changed anything between us in how we felt for each other. As far as going places, that's great. I'm happy for you. I'm leaving Key West soon myself to do the great loop then head over to Europe to go visit Jim Morrison's grave. You mentioned me working finally. Lol. Remember, I've done nothing but work every time you've ever seen me. You met me on post and then Sloppy Joe's. Lol. You didn't know about the other security job or other things I have going on. I've quit both of those jobs for you. So, remember facts and not what you add in to make it your reality. I loved you every minute. I still love you."

I'm not sure why, but I chatted with him back and forth a few more times. I think it was because I felt like I was in control for once. I knew what he'd done and what he was like, so why did I feel the need to text him? Was Chad still playing with me? I still felt like he could be that person I fell in love with. I still saw the good in him. I never told him I missed him; instead, I told him I missed the person I thought he was. I missed what could have been. He would tell me the same things that he used to say: that his soul missed me, how beautiful I was, that he missed my scent, and he just wanted to breathe me in. I told him I wasn't sure about all of that, only that he hurt me, and I could forgive, but I could never forget.

He'd tell me that he loved me, that every moment we had spent together was real. He said if I forget about him that's fine, but don't forget that he loved me. I told him I wanted to believe that he loved me at one point. He said he still loved me, and his soul loves my soul, not at one point in time, but all the time.

I couldn't understand why I was even texting him. What was wrong with me? I knew we would never be together again; he's not a good person and everyone's stories proved that. He hurt me something bad, and I deserve better, but there I was, texting him. Why did he have this hold over me? More importantly, why couldn't I break free?

Chad would tell me what I wanted to hear, and I knew that. It was all lies. I was weak. In order to move on, I couldn't keep doing this. I think I just wanted him to hurt as much as he hurt me. What I really wanted, more than anything else, was to hear him say he was sorry. I wanted him to feel bad that he hurt me. In my heart I knew I would never get that, and I knew I had to stop.

So, after that mess of a conversation, I decided it was time to finally block him for the last time. I would be closing this chapter again, for good. He couldn't hurt me anymore. Chad was not going to take my future, because I wasn't going to give it to him. It was time for me to move on and to not look back. He didn't deserve my thoughts and I didn't need to know where he was or what he was doing. The time I had with him was over.

A week went by, and it was finally November, when Julia and I had to say our goodbyes to Gainesville. Our thirteen-week contracts were up. We both moved back to our homes and went back to work at the hospitals we once left almost a year prior. We planned on seeing each other in the near future since we were only an hour and half away from each other. People come and go in your life for different reasons, and I believed Julia came into my life to stay. We had an amazing year in Florida as roommates, with lots of tears and laughter and fun. We were there for each other and we created a special bond.

This next year was going to be different: I was going to be near my girls, and soon I'd have another grandchild. This time, I would have a granddaughter! I was looking forward to being home. It was going to be a new year all around.

I planned to have a positive outlook on life and to always try new things. I wanted to continue with challenging myself to something new every year, or as often as I came up with new ideas. That wasn't very hard for me, if I'm being honest.

I went home to Seattle to be with my parents and brother and his family for Thanksgiving, and then I went on a seven-day cruise with a different ex-boyfriend in December. This one wasn't as crazy or a liar like Chad was. He was like my best friend and my comfort zone, and he had always been there for me in hard times or to support me on anything I did. I love him for that. We have a great connection and I know we would do anything for each other.

I did need something to keep my mind busy over the winter, though, besides work, so I decided my challenge for 2023 would be to take a 250+ hour yoga course. One of my daughters helped me sign up for it in January. It was intense, with long hours of studying, taking quizzes, researching, and writing essays, but I finally finished and passed with all 100's. It was a great accomplishment, and I would never have achieved that if I was with someone. I'm working on teaching classes at some point. My reward was taking a cruise by myself for four nights; another thing I would never have done if I was in a relationship. It was amazing, and now I am more confident to get out there and go and do, even if I am by myself. It was definitely time to focus on me and to do some self-reflecting.

Life can be scary and intimidating, but it is what you make it. It can be full of surprises. Sometimes you just have to take the leap and try something new. I can't wait to see what God has in store for me this next year. I do believe that when one chapter ends, another one begins, and this next chapter will definitely not involve a sailboat.

Epilogue

Life is about living and learning. I learned quite a bit last summer, even though a lot of it is still puzzling. For example: when I told my daughter about the maggots, she told me that they did a study in high school on decomposition, and it takes at least a week for maggots to get to the size I described to her. So, what was he doing during that time? He said it was just a few days.

Then there was that apartment he was at all the time saying it belonged to a buddy of his, but I'm pretty sure it was the woman he was probably driving around with in my truck. Maybe it was the red-headed girl the locals said he was seeing.

Of course, there was the boat on the dry dock on stilts. He never did send any pictures of it, and kept saying he was twenty grand in, then thirty. I don't think it was ever out of the water, and he definitely wasn't out that money. I noticed later that when he said it was out of the water, he sent a picture of an anchor he found that was on top of the boat, while the boat was in the water. I didn't put two and two together at the time. He kept thinking I would feel sorry for him and send him money. That was not going to happen. I gave enough as it was.

It should have been a clue when I asked if he had the military insurance Tricare and he answered with yes, he had three insurances. I remember being confused, but I never outright questioned him about it.

All the times he said he dropped his phone, had no charge on it, or when it was lost/stolen, he was probably with someone else. He led a double life and some locals saw it. I can't believe I fell for it every time when he mentioned something happening to his phone. Or maybe he had a second phone.

The HIV/AIDS pamphlets found on the boat that Clare mentioned threw me off guard. Who's were they? Maybe that's why the owner supposedly committed suicide? I was just glad my tests were all negative. If Chad really was seeing multiple women, I wouldn't blame him for wanting a pamphlet.

Who stole the bike from me? Was it him, was it his uncle? Did he convince someone to take it? Or was it someone else entirely?

I never did find out how Clare and Sam (the owners of the boat) found out where the boat was after it was towed into Marathon.

Did he even take the boat out on sea trials?

What about all the fights he was in? Was any of that true? Maybe he just had a great imagination.

Did he ever give his own bike to the boy, whose bike was stolen?

All the deaths. Did anyone really die, or did he make all that up too?

Where did he get the coral from?

I had a lot of unanswered questions and at one point I was obsessed with researching everything online. I had to stop. It wasn't healthy. Nothing was going to change because of it.

I learned that I should have read the book *'Sis, Don't Settle'* by Faith Jenkins years ago. It's a book about dating that I just finished reading. It made me realize everything I did wrong. I was too eager, wanting that instant gratification of love. I kept thinking why not me. You see it happen all the time, but do you see the end results? I wonder how many make it. We need to take the time to really get to know a person. Especially if they are from a different town and you don't know anything about them. Pay attention to the red flags and gut feelings. They are always right. Someone who talks too much about themselves could be a narcissist or selfish. Someone that tells too many stories could be trying to impress or put themselves in a higher light; they could also be wanting the attention all on themselves without giving anyone else a chance to talk. Someone who is always trying to impress you with their sweet talk and giving you attention, but then vanishes for hours or days at a time. Total red flags! Why didn't I see them? I really can't answer that. I was caught up in the moment and I let my guard down. It all sounded fun and exciting. It was all too good to be true, but I believed it was true.

I do believe everything is a learning experience. I came out unharmed, minus some money I spent on him. I had fun in Key West and enjoyed meeting all the locals. We had some good times and lots of laughter. I don't regret those moments, but I will use what I learned from the whole process to be a better person. I'm sure part of his childhood stories were real and that made him who he is today. That is no excuse to behave the way he did, but it makes me feel sorry for him in a way. I do believe in forgiveness and that is how I can move on. I can forgive him, but I will never forget.

After doing the podcast with Casey and talking to my dear friend named Mitch (who is a counselor/psychiatrist), I felt inspired to write this book and tell my story. Mitch has always been there for me with the most reassuring words and always at the right time. With his support and love, it made me want to help others at identifying red flags and gut feelings before it's too late. Talking to Mitch and doing the podcast was very encouraging.

I have a daily devotion that I get via my email, and this one in particular helped me confirm my feelings. This is what it said:

Only you can share your life message by Rick Warren

You don't have to be perfect to share your life message.

Did you know that God put you on Earth for a special reason? He wants to say something to the rest of the world through you. It's called your life message.

The Bible says in 1 Thessalonians 1:8, "Your lives are echoing the Master's Word...The news of your faith in God is out. We don't even have to say anything anymore - you're the message!" (The Message).

Any time you say, "This is what God's doing in my life," you're giving your life message. Any time you say, "I was praying about this, and here's what's happened," you've given a life message. Any time you say, "I've got this problem I'm struggling with, but God is helping me," you are sharing your life message. Only you can share your unique life message. Nobody else can do it for you. And if you don't share your life message, the world gets cheated.

God wants to use *you*. But why?

It's because the best messages are personal messages. The most powerful message comes through a person. I'm so glad that when God wanted to share his message of love, he didn't email it. He came in person. The Word became flesh. Jesus Christ came to Earth so we could see what God is like.

God has a message to share with the world, and instead of writing it in the sky, he wants to share it through your personality; he wants to share it through you.

You don't have to be perfect to share your life message. You just have to be honest, real, and authentic. Just say, "I don't have it all together, but here's what God is doing in my life. Here's the difference Jesus Christ has made." If you don't share your life message with other people, they may never hear about what God can do for them too.

Your life message is yours alone. No one else can share it. So, what will be the communication of your life?

After reading that devotion one day, it hit me like a rock. I knew then that I was supposed to tell my story. I am far from perfect, I make the biggest mistakes, and I definitely don't have it all together. But by telling my story of my mistakes, hopefully it will help someone else to not make the same ones.

I truly believe that God was watching over me and helped me to get out of what could have been a really bad situation. I was praying and praying for Him to show me what I needed to do because my gut was in knots, telling me that something wasn't right. It was that next morning when I noticed the anonymous tip. He gave me a sign. I may have ignored prior signs and did what I wanted to, but I saw that sign on that particular day.

John 8:32 says, "And you shall know the truth, and the truth will set you free." I was seeking the truth through prayers and the next day they were answered. It was not what I wanted to hear, but it was what I needed to hear. The truth can be abrasive sometimes but is very essential.

Through this experience, I also learned that it's easy to fall back in the same situation, hoping that the person you love will change, because you see the good in them. I did that by texting Chad when I shouldn't have. I saw the good in him, or at least I thought I did, but he will never change. I know now why women in abusive relationships go back to the ones they love after being abused by them, and that abuse takes many forms. A lot of abuse is silent, not the physical kind most people tend to think about. We

270

see that good person deep down, the one we fell in love with. It's hard to walk away from that.

I learned that we need to not judge someone for something that we haven't gone through ourselves. The best we can do for someone is to be there for them, even if we don't understand. Life is hard, and we get weak. Trying to end or stop the cycle is not easy and it takes time, with many ups and downs, victories, and mistakes. How many times did I "officially" block Chad, just to unblock him within a month or two? I finally decided to do the right thing for me, for good, and let it go and block him with no turning back. That last time was very solidifying and satisfying because I knew for a fact that I was not going back.

It's been over a year, and I think I'm finally ready: ready to put it all behind me, to stop the researching, and to let it be. There's nothing left except to thank Chad for the experience. And to thank him for a book I never would have written, which is also the closure I needed.

I'm not sure what lies ahead for me. I still believe in true love and soulmates. I know that God has the perfect man out there for me, I just need to be patient and take my time. Even though a year has passed, I'm still not sure when I'll have the courage to date again. I get lonely, but I'm a little apprehensive about going out, and I know that being lonely is no reason to jump into the next relationship.

I know I'm worth the wait, and I'm not going to be doing the chasing anymore. I will continue to do the things I enjoy. I have learned a lot about myself and my mistakes. I'm learning to trust in the Lord first and let Him lead my way instead of me taking the wheel and going in the wrong direction. His plan for me may not be my plan for me, which is sometimes hard to swallow, even though I know His plan is full of hope, love, peace, and contentment, plus so much more. I'm learning to love myself first. I'm a strong independent woman and I know my worth. I will not play games; life is too short.

I'm still a dreamer and I will keep traveling and experiencing life to the fullest while I can. I will try to live by my words and to be a better person, but I do get weak and make mistakes, nobody is perfect. The least we can do is try.

Life is meant to be enjoyed whether it's by yourself or with friends. It all starts with a positive attitude. We live and learn by our mistakes. If I can help others along the way, either by sharing my mistakes, being an encourager, believing in prayer, or by just being me, then it's all been worth the journey.

We all have a story to tell, so write the book! Tell your story! Share what you know! If I can do it (and I'm by no means a writer, nor was I any good in English class), so can you! You could help someone change their life if you do.

The greatest glory in living

lies not in never falling,

But in rising every time we fall

-Nelson Mandela

About the Author

Kimberly Rae Owens is 58 and resides in Madison, Alabama. She has 3 daughters, 2 grandkids, and one grand puppy.

She is a respiratory therapist at the local hospital and enjoys helping others, woodworking, yoga, reading, exercising, spending time with family and friends, learning new things, and always enjoys planning her next trip. She has the desire to travel solo more often with the inspiration from the women on the Facebook group called 'Solo in Style; Women over 50 traveling solo & loving it'.

She still has the dream to have a place near a beach and to rent something out for Airbnb, and to be an influencer or encourager of some sort, maybe even teach yoga with mimosas on the beach.

She is listening more to God, her gut and others and has her heart open to what God's plan may be, knowing it may be entirely different than hers.

She continues to smile, be positive, and to make the most of each day. She is always looking for a new challenge or next adventure in hopes that it will teach her girls that you can do anything you put your mind to, whether you do it solo or not, and to show them and others you are never too old to try new things.